HOW TO TAKE TROUT ON WET FLIES AND NYMPHS

HOW TO TAKE TROUT ON WET FLIES AND NYMPHS

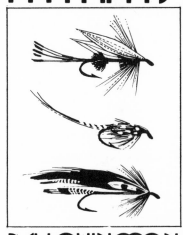

RAY OVINGTON

 FRESHET PRESS   ROCKVILLE CENTRE, NEW YORK

ISBN 088395–020–0

Library of Congress catalog card number: 72–92786

Manufactured in the United States of America

Designed by John Reale

Illustrations by George Meyerriecks

To the Brotherhood of the Angle—
past, present and future

CONTENTS

Foreword	ix
Introduction	xiii
Tackle Talk	1
Fishing the Wet Fly	27
The Sport of Nymph Fishing	79
It's Fun to Tie Flies	145
Striking, Playing and Landing	161
A Stream of Thoughts and Memories	175

Foreword

Anglers and those who appreciate angling literature can be thankful for the present upswing of interest in angling books. Many new and old classics have been reprinted, and some fine new titles are appearing each season. For many years I've collected angling books. My book, *Angling Literature,* Sultana Press, 1970, lists a part of my personal collection of some twenty-four hundred volumes. In 1969 I donated my collection to California State College at Fullerton, and it is now being enlarged and well preserved at the college. In the collection is a copy of Ray Ovington's *How to Take Trout on Wet Flies and Nymphs,* 1952, Boston, Little, Brown and Company.

In my collection I've tried to separate the wheat from the chaff, and the effort has required much burning of midnight oil, toiling through some books, completely enjoying others. I ran across the first edition of *How to Take Trout* some years ago. It has since become a classic. It deals with the insects common to trout streams in a manner somewhat similar to that of Preston Jennings and Art Flick. Like them, Ray offers many trout-taking patterns and goes into the necessary details of tying the artificials, but what is even more important, he doesn't leave you there, for he also elucidates the indispensible matters of streamcraft and presentation, essential elements in fly fishing if the entomological facts are to be put to practical use. It was one of the first and is still one of the few detailed books on this aspect of fly fishing.

But where was Ray Ovington, I wondered, and what was he like? Since the first edition of this book appeared he had written and illustrated a number of books, among them the outstandingly successful *Tactics on Trout,* 1969, Alfred Knopf, which has become a selection of the critical Outdoor Life Book Club.

Then, as if it had been prearranged, Ovington appeared on the scene out here in southern California. I met him and had several talks with him. Since then we have become good friends. It would be good, I thought, to see *How to Take Trout* back in print and available to the many new anglers who have appeared on the scene since it was first published in 1952. In a chance conversation with Dr. Myron Cohen of Freshet Press, I found that he, too, had a high regard for the book. It was then only a matter of bringing the two parties together to decide how the book could be up-dated, revised, and enlarged in the light of Ray's more than twenty years of additional experience in the art of wet-fly fishing.

Ray writes and illustrates with a background that is unusual in the angling field. He is a devout angler, a tireless experimenter, and an able reporter, having held responsible positions in advertising, radio, and TV, as well as having been a magazine editor, a writer for outdoor and sport magazines, and a daily outdoor newspaper columnist. He is the author-illustrator of some twenty books on the outdoors.

Many anglers have knowledge but cannot or do not put their knowledge into print. Many writers have a gifted pen but lack the experience of a lifetime of experimental angling. Ray Ovington has both qualities, and this work in particular will hold the attention of the most fastidious reader and avid fisherman. Certainly the expert fly tier will have some new horizons opened to him in these pages, for they offer some extremely valuable new patterns.

Any angler who has read *Tactics on Trout* will appreciate a new edition of *How to Take Trout*. It is with a high regard and my best wishes that I recommend it to expert and novice alike. It will give the reader a broad insight into both the insect life of trout streams and the often puzzling behavior of trout. I consider it to be the finest general introduction to wet-fly and nymph fishing. I'm sure it will give you as much pleasure in the reading as it will profit on the stream.

—Mark Kerridge,
Vice-President of The Federation
of Fly Fishers

Introduction

After completing *Tactics on Trout* and *Tactics on Bass,* I
said to Angus Cameron, my editor at Alfred Knopf,
"There, you've had it. I don't see how I can ever write
another book on angling. I've said everything I have to
say." Then came the prospect of revising *How to Take
Trout on Wet Flies and Nymphs.* Could I add anything
fresh and new to the old book? I decided that I could, for
I'd much enlarged my field of study, especially in the West,
had painstakingly catalogued my findings, and had
developed many fish-taking nymph and wet-fly patterns
since 1952, when *How to Take Trout* was first published.
When Dr. Myron Cohen of Freshet Press spoke to me
about a revision and reprint, I stipulated that along with
revising the text and adding new material, I'd also like to
write a concluding chapter of reflections and reminis-

cences, even though they had nothing to do with fly-fishing techniques. I hope you will enjoy this new chapter, which I've called "A Stream of Thoughts and Memories."

Like so many serious anglers, I've developed a keen desire to promote fishing through how-to writing as a means of helping novice sportsmen get to know and respect the outdoors and to do whatever they can to preserve it for future generations. I believe that even the authors of how-to fishing books write with the thought in mind of opening their readers' eyes and hearts to our great natural heritage.

This book, then, along with my others, is written with the hope of causing the angler to sharpen his eyes, ears, and wits in order to penetrate the vagaries of the current and the other mysteries of the natural world. It is also meant to encourage the reader to be mindful of the natural causes and effects that constitute the world we live in and from which our physical bodies have arisen. As Izaak Walton said, "There is more to fishing than to fish."

As I roll back the memory tape to 1950, and then run it forward, I find myself reflecting on a host of changes and developments in sport fishing in America. After the boom of its early years, spinning has leveled off as a well-entrenched fishing method. It has been responsible for introducing fishing to an entire generation, many members of which have branched out and taken up fly fishing, some even turning to fly fishing exclusively for the fullest enjoyment of trout. The population has exploded, and the new generation shows promise of developing an entirely sport-minded clan of anglers whose concern with conservation is greater and more intense than that of the generations which preceded them.

This increased interest in fishing is reflected in the sale

and library readership of fishing books, for, as well as being a time of increasing field experience in sport angling, recent years have also seen a remarkable upswing of interest in angling educational materials. Fishing clubs are gaining in number, and the younger members are beginning to outrank the old-timers. Organizations such as Trout Unlimited and The Federation of Fly Fishers are not concerned with the machinations of a few old codgers. They have big nationwide memberships and are actively approaching the steps of Capitol Hill.

When the fly-fishing-only idea was barely getting started back in 1950, its proponents had a hard row to hoe, but today fly-fishing-only waters and even no-kill areas and barbless hooks are being readily accepted by a large percentage of anglers who prefer to release their trout.

Dry-fly fishing, once thought of as the highest form of purist angling, has grown in its number of devotees, and so has wet-fly and nymph fishing. Those who converted from spinning to fly fishing often started with the dry fly because drifting flies on the surface is an easier way of learning to fly fish, since in dry-fly fishing both the fly and the strike can always be seen. Now, some of these anglers are finding out that there is much more of keen interest *below* the surface of the water. This subsurface world can be reached and enjoyed by the use of wet flies, nymphs, and streamers. Those who pursue this aspect of fly fishing find that it is as deadly as bait fishing, perhaps even deadlier when it comes to numbers of strikes and netted fish. This is the time the conservation bug sets in. One would hardly employ a barbless hook when bait fishing, but it is being done with increasing frequency by fly fishermen.

No two streams are alike; no two pools on a river are ever alike; no single pool or stretch of water is ever the same twice; and certainly trout often change their behavior from hour to hour. However, there are basic conditions that bring about specific actions on the part of the trout, and when these conditions are recognized, trout behavior can be predicted and certain techniques can be brought to bear under almost all circumstances. Trout, like people, have certain habit patterns that they conform to. Knowing these patterns in relation to momentary conditions in the trout's environment is the key to successful angling. The main purpose of this book is to show the reader how these conditions can be recognized and what techniques should be employed in a given situation.

In the final chapter, I ask your attention during the passages that concern conservation and the need for a defined public policy in the preservation and improvement of our natural resources. This is coming about gradually, amid harsh growing pains. Things will only get better when they get bad enough for all to realize that the possible end of life on our planet is a growing threat. As usual, it is the sportsmen who are the most ardent, the most dedicated, and the most field-informed sponsors of protective and preventive measures. (Audubon had to shoot his birds in order to paint them. The official Audubon Society picture shows John from the chest up, conveniently eliminating the shotgun resting in his lap.) The sportsman proudly holds up his rod or gun and states emphatically that game is a crop —and as such is different from other forms of wildlife—to be cultivated by scientific conservation measures and harvested within the bounds of reason. He will fight for the right to hunt and fish and for the preservation of the natural resources that provide him with those rights. He knows that if the game and fish go, man's demise is not far behind.

But I am preaching, so let's drop the subject until the last chapter. Now let's go fishing!

Before we wade in, I would like to again offer my thanks to Jim Deren of the Angler's Roost in New York for starting me out as an outdoor writer; to Angus Cameron for his editorial labors over the years; and to Mark Kerridge for encouraging this present effort.

HOW TO TAKE TROUT ON WET FLIES AND NYMPHS

CHAPTER I
Tackle Talk

Selecting the Fly Rod

Buying fishing tackle is a lot of fun—and the study of tackle and fishing requirements is an important element in the complete enjoyment of angling. Take my advice and leave your checkbook at home on your first visit to the tackle store. When a fellow angler or the sales clerk points out materials, markings, a quality or type of ferrule, or begins to discuss the actions of various rods, make certain mental reservations. Then go alone to several tackle shops and examine the stock without looking at the price tags, simply as a check up on your powers of evaluation. Look at the dollar sign only after you have thoroughly inspected the rod and have tried its action. When you have narrowed your choice to two or three rods, with definite reasons for the choice, you are getting somewhere. Remember that your first rod will not be your sole lifetime purchase. After forty-odd years of fishing, I still flex rods in tackle shops in an attempt to find *the* rod of my choice.

The reasons for this continuing hunt are many. Virtually any decent rod will suffice at first, and with proper care and legitimate use it will last many seasons. A hundred-dollar rod in the hands of a tyro will probably perform little better than one costing a third that, though may I warn against buying too cheap a rod as your initial purchase, for that is worse than an extravagance—it is a serious detriment to learning and enjoying the pleasures of angling.

Before selecting that first rod, or any rod for that matter, it's a good idea to examine some of the existing fallacies and stubborn superstitions that tend to mislead. Here are some points to consider.

Tradition has it that bamboo is the only material possessing the required life and action. Twenty years ago this supposition was correct, but today one can buy excellent rods made of spun glass. While these rods do not have the same *type* of action that is found in bamboo, they are more than adequate on the stream, in the hands of the right man. Their definite advantages over bamboo are that they are relatively inexpensive, they will not take a "set," and their ferrules will not come loose. These rods will stand the strain of rough handling and require little care.

Anglers talk a good deal about the lightness of their rods, but just because a rod is light in weight does not mean it possesses a finer action than one that weighs somewhat more. For one thing, the weight of the handle and reel seat, not to mention the guides and ferrules, enters the picture. A rod that is exceptionally light cannot have the strength and durability of a heavier one, though a rod that weighs more does not necessarily have as fast or strong an action as it should for the amount it weighs.

You get what you pay for in quality. A fifty-dollar bamboo stick may appear similar to a hundred-dollar one in the tackle store, but look closely. Study the manufacturer's catalogue and the details of rod construction. When you know what you are paying for you will have confidence in and respect for your purchase.

Not long ago I fished with several members of the Wilderness Fly Fishers' Club on the famed Kings River in California. These gentlemen were all knowledgeable anglers of the technically minded sort who study rod actions and types of lines and micrometer all their leaders. I was sure I could learn from them, and they seemed to think they could learn something from me.

We first spent several hours in an informal casting clinic and rod-selection session. We also attacked several of the stream-situation problems outlined in various chapters of my books. During that weekend I fished with nine different rods with lines that had been chosen by the rods' owners. It was an interesting test of my ability to adjust to a wide variety of rod actions. Cliff Wyatt's rods were the most difficult to get used to, though they are superb glass rods. His basic design incorporates a very stiff, large-diameter butt tapering quickly to a midsection and tip of very fast action. To cast well with these rods, a very stiff wrist is needed. The cast involves the shoulder and back as well as the arm. On the long doublehaul casts I found my right foot being almost lifted off the ground. Yet with all their stiffness, I found I could use them with less total effort than I had to put out with the more whippy rods that I tried that weekend. But to handle a Wyatt, one has to learn the rod's characteristics and adapt to them. They reminded me of the first Edwards Quadrates in bamboo, which were as stiff as pokers.

I relate this incident here in order to prompt the reader to assess his own casting habits before buying a rod. Consider your timing and mannerisms—your casting personality—and then look for a rod that is suitable for your style of casting. To arbitrarily buy a rod of a specific type of action and to then try to adapt to it can be a difficult and frustrating business. You should know what sort of rod suits you best before you buy a specific type of rod. If you're an absolute beginner, this poses a problem that only a certain amount of experience can remedy.

The discussion over the basic types of rods has been going on for eons, and I doubt that anyone will ever really settle the argument. Some experts think they have the answers for everyone, but most writings on the subject of rod actions resemble treatises on women—but in the last analysis, there's no substitute for experience. During the question-and-answer session at that same club meeting, someone asked why and under which conditions one should choose either a whippy "wet-fly" action or a stiffer "dry-fly" action. I countered with a series of questions, theories, and problems of my own. First, is such a rod distinction necessary, and if so, how do you define it?

One theory has it that a stiff-tipped rod working a very fine tippet, say a 7X, will set the hook much too quickly and forcefully, whether one is using a dry fly or a nymph. Sounds logical, but is it true? Most of the time in upstream dry-fly fishing and in most nymph fishing there is a generous amount of slack line involved. If the angler has learned to use his line as a bobber and keeps his rod at right angles to the line when it is drifting, the stiff tip will allow a faster and more definite strike. But a stiff-action rod equipped with a weight-forward taper will not perform well under forty feet, which is the range usually chosen by both nymph and dry-fly fishermen. Such a rig is meant to perform well from fifty feet out. And it doesn't roll cast well. The proponents of soft-action, soft-tip rods believe that a slower action is best for shorter casts, roll casts, accurate targeting, and softer striking, even though a more powerful back-hand might be needed to gather the slack before the hook is set into the fish.

These questions also have a bearing on the preferred rod length, since a rod's dimensions have much to do with its action. There are anglers of my acquaintance who swear by six-foot rods, and I've seen them handle long and short casts with tremendous efficiency. Then, there's the long-rod school, which contends that in order to control the line on the water, a long rod held high is the only way to allow a drift if there is fast water between you and the strip of water you want to fish. Some prefer a fast-action long rod for this; others are happy only with a long, slow stick. And some men like short rods with fast action.

Theories, theories—and all valid, or partially so, at least to the people whose ideas of what a rod should be are more or less in agreement with what their favorite rods are like. And where do these speculations leave us? Right where we started.

The selection of the proper rod must be based on the personality of the angler, his physical power, and the degree of timing and control that he can exert over his casting. Though no one rod can fit everybody, there *is* one rod that will fit the individual when he has weighed all the theories in actual practice. Once the angler has that rod, he can fish well with it, despite the fact that his partner uses one of an entirely different action.

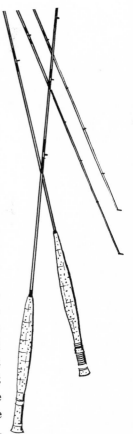

Sometimes a "perfect" rod comes as an accident. In my dad's collection was a soft and whippy old Hardy. You could feel the action of that rod right down into the handle. The tip section was so thin that it was scary even to look at. That was the softest tip I'd ever fished with. Eventually it acquired a bad set that I could not work out. Finally it broke. I hated to retire the old rod, so I looked everywhere for a tip section that would fit it. Finally I located a store that had some extra bamboo tip sections. During World War II, this sort of thing was especially difficult to find. At that point I was ready to settle for any tip and ferrule that would fit, regardless of the resultant action. When I put the new tip section on the old rod and waved it to feel the action, I was in for a shock. I'd never felt anything like it.

The whole rod seemed to wave as if in a stiff breeze. I wondered what it would cast like. I grabbed a reel with a weight-forward line and began casting, stripping line as I lengthened the cast. The rod's action was very slow and almost willowy, but it kept straining for more line. Now with almost all of the line in the air, I stripped off some backing and away it went. That rod would cover any stream situation I could envision. I showed it to many anglers who laughed at it until they cast with it. Then when Charles Ritz was in New York, I discussed this rod with him. It seemed, way back then, that he was experimenting with that same kind of action. I had stumbled by accident on the same sort of design that Charles was developing by careful experiments.

The search for that perfect rod can go on for years and years as one's needs change. I can remember at least twenty rods that I've owned over the years, starting with the Hardy and other imported bamboo rods that were part of my father's collection. I've gone through some good American rods too, including the famed Nat Uslan five-strip rods, which were absolutely superb. I've haunted the William Mills store in New York City and have talked with the rod builders at their factory and suggested specific tapers. I've gone from bamboo to glass and back to bamboo and back to glass. Now I'm back to glass, for it has come a long way since those early days.

My most romantic marriage with a fly rod happened when I was living in New York before World War II. I was broke, but I wanted to buy a rod that would be my pride and joy for the years to come. I'd been through many rods, and I thought I was ready to settle for a really good one. It would cost money, but I was bound and determined. I walked into the dusty and musty Mills store across the street from the Woolworth Building. This was the very first tackle store in New York and the one patronized by the much-touted members of the New York Anglers Club. I talked to Arthur Mills and to Dick Wolff, who was then a clerk in the store. I plunked down a miserable down payment, and by the time of the next trout season I owned a Mills bamboo rod. It was a gentle-looking fly rod eight feet long—all one piece. It was made of six unbroken strips of bamboo. When I first saw it I hardly dared touch it. Then Arthur asked me to pick it up. I went into immediate raptures.

I guess I loved that one-piece rod more than all the rest, even though it fell short of some glass rods developed since. I took it along on many trips and used it for everything —tiny spinners, multiple wet flies, single weighted nymphs, and dry flies. It was also an excellent rod for midge fishing with the very smallest flies.

One day I was fishing with John Lowell Pratt, the one-time editor of the Barnes Sports Library, which published the famed dollar series of sports books. Lowell and I had done a flock of books together. I waded up to him and asked him to try the rod and see how it cast for him. He immediately went into the same sort of raptures that I had felt the day when Arthur had shown the rod to me. So the rod changed hands, then and there.

A few years later, Lowell and I were dining near his office off Madison Avenue. He reminded me of that day on the Beaverkill. Then he told me he had cancer and that his days were numbered. He didn't know whether he'd live to fish another season. He didn't, but I've the feeling that wherever that good being has gone there must be a place for him to use that rod. He was a fine man, a credit to the brotherhood of angling and sports publishing.

So boiling it all down, the selection of a rod and a balancing line and leader is a matter of fitting the rod to your own personality. You are your own expert, and that title can only come from experience.

Balance—the Angler

In order to effectuate a perfect working team of rod, reel, line, leader and angler, we must first take into consideration the angler. The reason for this is to ascertain the amount of physical strength, coordination, and sensitiveness he possesses.

One angler of my acquaintance weighs over two hundred pounds and stands six feet above the shore line. He was right end on his college football team, yet this big fellow is as gentle as a mayfly on the stream. While we were out fishing one day, my wife suggested he try her little seven-and-a-half-foot Hardy that weighs a hair over two ounces. I had some misgivings as to what might happen, but he handled that rod more gently than my wife, who I assure you is half his size and has a tenth of his strength.

Another day, at the sailboat pool of Central Park in New York City, I chanced upon an angler trying out a new rod. This, too, was a light seven-and-a-half-foot rod, bearing the Thomas signature. The man was small and slight, and after a few trial casts he decided to see how far this wand could throw the line. He was using a line suitable for an eight-and-a-half-foot, five-ounce rod, and that was his first mistake. I cautioned him, but he went right on.

Out and back shot the line, a nice sight as it sailed through the air. Gradually he stripped more line and the rod seemed to be handling it all right, though the casting now required more effort and longer pauses to straighten out the length.

"Better stop there," I called.

"I should say not. This beauty will throw another twenty feet," he returned.

I stepped some distance away, scarcely daring to look at the bend of the rod, which by now was handling far too much weight. On one of the forward throws, the owner pushed too much and I heard the inevitable snap of the bamboo fiber. The rod broke just below the second ferrule.

I have cited these two instances to point out that physical prowess alone should not determine the choice of rod or enter into the business of arriving at balanced tackle. It is the judgment and personality of the angler that must be the first determining factor in the choice and size of rod to be used comfortably under normal fishing conditions. Naturally, steelhead and salmon fishing require heavier tackle, but I speak here of normal stream-trout fishing where trout larger than twenty inches are exceedingly rare.

Take a glance at almost any angler on the stream and you'll see immediately why so many rods of superior design and quality end up in the graveyard so quickly. There is the dry-fly angler who furiously whips his rod back and forth in false casts, making the leader whistle and sing in the air. (It is of course necessary to false cast with power to dry the fly, but usually the dry-fly man false casts too long a line too hard and for too long a time.) This will kill the fibers in any bamboo rod, no matter how fine the bamboo or how perfect the rod's design. The simple fact is that bamboo fibers weaken with use, quicker with overuse. Most modern dry-fly rods are fashioned to shoot the line. False cast, sure, but with a short line and a minimum of power. Coil the extra shooting line in the free hand, and when the line's pointed toward the target add power to the last forward drive.

To save the precious rod fibers, learn to pick the line off the water easily. When the line has drifted well below, let it swing around in the current to a point where it can be effortlessly hand retrieved. Raise the rod tip, bringing the fly and leader on or near the top of the water. Lift and false cast toward the desired run and again shoot the line forward. To retrieve while the fly is still above you or to the side in the current, strip in the line until there is little left drifting on the water and throw the rod forward in a modified roll cast. The line and then the fly will be lifted up and out of the water with a minimum of flurry. While the fly is in the air, pull back and false cast as usual preparatory to making the next throw. Incidentally, a gentle pick-up will not only save your rod and wrist but will also help to eliminate surface disturbance.

The confirmed distance caster regularly works fifty or sixty feet of line and expects his rod to stand up under the strain hour after hour. If he uses heavy bucktails or a brace of wet flies or nymphs, perhaps with a weighted leader, the death of the rod's action will only be hastened.

Remember, too, that nothing wears out a rod more than continual slapping of the fly or line on the back cast. When this does happen, one of several things may be causing it. There may be a knot in the line that is breaking the even flow of the cast, or perhaps there is a bit of slime on the leader knots. More often than not, however, the slapping comes from casting fatigue and carelessness. Rest a minute and compose yourself, and above all, remember to keep the rod from going far beyond the vertical position on the back portion of the cast. This will keep your line working high in the air and will help to eliminate slapping, sloppy work.

Spinner fishing with a light fly rod is one of the quickest ways to ruin a delicate rod. Help save the rod by bringing the spinner to the top of the water before attempting to lift it into the air for a recast. Obviously, much false casting with even a tiny spinner is guaranteed to wreck *any* rod in time. Split shot or wrap-around lead and a glob of worms schedules the recessional almost as quickly. The fly rod was never designed to cast a weight of any kind other than the line and flies of normal size. There are, of course, fly rods that will take these heavy rigs, but you will find them mostly unsuitable for delicate fly work.

Though most of us usually handle our rods with care, we are apt to slide into the bad habit of straining them. This usually occurs when the fishing is good or excitement stimulates us into a frenzy of action. Then there is a tendency to overwork the arm and wrist in the belief that this will increase the distance of the cast. Failure to allow the line to straighten out at the end of the sweep will require more pressure on the forward and backward swing than is advisable or necessary. The cast will not level off when it is released, and the final result is a hard fall of the lure and leader on the water, or worse still, only a short distance covered with an accompanying sloppy delivery of slack line.

With proper handling, my wife's little seven-and-a-half-foot, two-ounce Hardy easily reaches out forty feet or more. Helen has used this rod for three years but until recently has not only overworked herself, but the rod as well. She has finally come to realize that casting with this dainty little stick should be a dainty, smooth operation. She has learned to allow the line to straighten out fully on the back cast before starting the forward throw. There is a subtle feel that comes to a person who is learning to become a really good caster, and once the sensation of line pressure and balance is felt, timing of the cast becomes a much easier proposition.

One afternoon Roger and I got to talking about rods and actions and he produced a nine-foot rod that he seldom uses because, he said, the rod is too heavy and takes too much energy to cast all day.

When he put the rod together and threaded the guides with tapered line, I asked if I might try it. I false cast over the grass, lengthening the line to get the feel of the stick. Stripping some eight feet of additional line, I released the cast forward and the line shot out with a powerful zip, causing the reel to buzz. I recast again and when approximately forty feet of line was in the air, stripped another twenty and held this in my hand. The line shot forward and again the reel clicked as if it were asking for more. When I reeled in, Roger came over wearing an expression of almost stupefied amazement.

"Roger, this a beautiful rod—darned if I'd call it heavy; why, I could use this one all day."

Roger then started to false cast and immediately I saw why he was having trouble. With only thirty feet of line in the air, he was using enough power to reach out seventy.

"Take it easy," I advised. "Slow down your timing. The line isn't straightening out behind. Give it more time and cut down on your drive."

At about half his original speed and power, he was still using too much, so I went over behind him and grasped his rod handle. He had a veritable death grip on it, and his arm was tense and trembling, the veins standing out in high relief. Asking him to merely hold the rod, I cast it for him, slowing down the swing and easing up on the pressure until the line was sailing back and forth with rhythmic ease.

"There, Roger," I said, "there's your trouble. You are still casting the same amount of line, yet now you are using one quarter the power and have slowed down too. There's nothing wrong with the rod; let it do what it was designed for." .

Incidentally, Roger had wanted to sell me the rod a few minutes before, but rescinded the offer.

Friends of mine who view the many rods in my collection ask how I can adapt to each one of them and how I get used to one type action and switch to another without many hours of readjustment. I point out that the readjustment can be accomplished in the first few false casts, when it is possible to get the rod's feel. From then on, it is merely a matter of staying with the rod and its action. I find it a great relief to switch rods often during an extended fishing trip, for I enjoy the change of pace.

Since no two rods are alike in action or weight, the owner must learn to use his rod and get acquainted with its specific peculiarities of speed and power.

It pays to observe the rod handling of a really good caster, when you can locate one on the stream. You will find that the angler is poised and relaxed. The entire movement is a smooth synchronization of body, arm, and wrist. It is a beautiful sight to watch the rod flash in the light, sending the line in a graceful bow through the air. Finally, at the peak of the motion, the great long line of light straightens out well behind the angler one second and in front of him the next. The climax comes when the forward throw stops the line just above the water and the fly lands gently. The angler then readies himself for come what may. There is a particular satisfaction in performing well, and whether or not the fish are rising, a profound confidence comes with having mastered the fine art of casting.

Balance—Rod and Line

In years gone by, the usual system for arriving at the proper line taper and weight of line was by its relationship to the weight of the rod. In those days there were few variations in action, most rods being of the whippy or semi-whippy type, so this method worked fairly well. But today, this system does not apply, owing to the advent of a wide variety of rod actions for rods of the same weight. A general rule would be to govern the line selection to fit the relative stiffness, power, and speed of the rod in question, remembering that the stiffer, faster-action rod requires a heavier tapered line but the slow or soft-action rod will handle a lighter line under most circumstances. Many glass rods will work well with two or even three different line weights.

I have been accused of being too much of a specialist. I own ten reels and each has a different line on it, and when I take to the stream with a particular rod, I sometimes carry three reels along and change them often if the situation demands. This may sound a little silly to some, but the pleasures of angling are many and varied. I like to be able to perform at my very best, and because I am not in a great rush to cover all the water and catch all the fish, I am content to wade ashore or sit on a rock and change reels.

There are two basic types of lines—level and tapered. I think it obvious that the best fly casting is done with the tapered line, and the difference in price between it and the level line is well worth it, even as an initial investment by a beginner. The tapered point on double-tapered lines serves the function of delivering the cast gently on the surface. However, if you use extremely long leaders, of at least fifteen feet or more, and put the taper in the leader, a level line will suffice, unless you are attempting casts of fifty feet or more. A weight forward line is needed for distance casting.

Lines are manufactured in silk, dacron, and nylon. An angler's preference for one or the other is usually marked and for very good reasons. Each has its decided advantages—and drawbacks.

For most people, the best all-round line is a nylon floater. Nylon lines are durable, widely available, require little care, and are virtually unsinkable under normal conditions. Nevertheless, I'd like to put in a good word for the old-fashioned silk lines. Though they are difficult to come by nowadays, a few experienced anglers continue to swear by them. If you should chance to find a source of supply and are curious about how these old favorites perform, here are a few comments on their properties.

A good silk line will last for years, though it must have constant and ever-loving care. This requires wiping it dry after each use and rubbing it tenderly with a preservative wax. This will protect the finish and also keep it waterproof and high floating. No line will stand up for long if snagged by brush or walked on by chains or brogues, nor will it survive long after being carelessly dragged over rocks, rough edges, or gunwales.

Nylon lines will float indefinitely with little or no dressing or care. They do not mildew nor will they kink and form breaks which materially weaken their over-all strength. There is a very definite difference in the "feel" between nylon and silk lines in casting, even though weight factors are well equalized by the difference in prescribed size. My silk lines throw a straighter cast with less effort, and the shooting quality of silk lines is the cause of my preference.

The proper way to put a silk fly line on the reel without starting out with a twist is an important first step. First, line up the coil with the reel and then attach the line to the reel spool, or the end of the backing line that is already on the spool. Have someone do the reeling for you and as this is done, slowly revolve the coil as the line is pulled by the reel. This is not a quick way to put it on, but is the right way, to eliminate any twist. *Never* reel in the line from a flat coil position or it will take its initial twist as each circle of line goes onto the spool.

If a line does become twisted either by faulty handling or by constant use and retrieving, the best way to straighten it out is to select a stretch of fast water and strip all line off the reel and let it float downstream. The action of the current will gradually eliminate the twists.

Do not pull out a loop or twist. If you do, the finish will fracture where the line doubles and crosses itself—thus beginning a weak spot, a place for damaging water to enter and start rot. Dressing these spots will ward off the evil day, but it pays to avoid these bruises of the finish as much as possible.

Never leave the line packed on the reel for any length of time or it will become sticky and tacky—the first step toward ruin. When this does happen, the best thing to do, if it is not too bad, is wash it thoroughly in a very mild solution of castile soap, or detergent, in lukewarm water. Hang it up to dry on wooden pegs, not nails. When it's bone dry, apply dressing liberally, working it into the line strenuously with the fingers. Let it dry in coils. If it is still tacky, the finish has gone beyond this stage of repair.

During the past few years some excellent sinking fly lines have appeared on the market. Now, risking the accusation of being a fuddy duddy, I want to remind you that for more than a hundred years anglers have been trying to find a line that would *float* well. Now that we've found that, we want to *sink* our lines! O.K., you can have your sinking lines, and I hope you are happy. I still prefer a floating line, even for deep nymph fishing. It picks up off the water better, faster, and easier, and it acts as a bobber when the trout are hitting light. If I have to fish deeper than a twelve-foot leader will sink in the current, I'll switch to dynamite.

Balance—the Leader

For best results the proper leader for wet-fly fishing, especially over "touchy" trout, should be at least nine-feet long, gradually tapered from heavy where it joins the line down to 2X for extra-heavy fishing (bucktails). Tippets of 6X and 7X are needed for very small flies and nymphs, especially when surface fishing, where the leader is in silhouette. A 4X tippet is satisfactory for flies in sizes 10, 12, and 14.

The best balance of rod and line can be completely upset by a too light, short or long leader. A heavy line tip with too light a butt section in the leader will not cast well. A light line tip with a long light leader is worse. A torpedo taper with a fine tip and too light and long a leader is a complete abomination. To effectuate the proper balance the leader should become theoretically, and actually, the tapered extension of the line. If it were not for the necessity of leaders, a fly line designed to taper to, say, 4X would be just about perfect. Since we cannot have this, we must strive for a leader that balances with the line. Length and taper design of the leader are as important as the taper of the line and the action of the rod.

A good general principle to follow is the sixty/forty rule. This means that the first sixty percent of the leader (the butt section) should be quite heavy, while the remaining forty percent should be much lighter. This last forty percent should be divided into two nearly equal sections—a sharp taper and the tippet. Most good-quality commercial leaders now follow this general formula. Leaders not of this type will almost always fail to straighten properly.

Reels For Fly-Fishing

The first and main function of a reel is to hold the line. Casting, hooking, and playing the fish require only the reel's ability to release line drawn from it by hand, or in the case of exceptionally big fish, to release line evenly and surely as the fish pulls it out.

Many fly reels are equipped with an adjustable drag which can be set at any point from free-spooling (the near absence of drag) all the way to a pressure that makes it difficult to strip off line. Many anglers rely on this drag for striking and playing the fish, having preset the tension to just under the breaking point of the leader as tested on the rod when bent.

Fly-rod reels come in various sizes designed to accept the many lengths and diameters of level and tapered lines. For ordinary trout fishing, I suggest that you buy one which will take the standard tapered fly line of thirty-yard length, plus allowance for backing. It is seldom that you will need this additional backing, but when you do, you'll be glad it is there. When you buy a reel, make absolutely sure that it will hold your line and leave ample space on the spool for loose winding. The quickest way to lose a fish or ruin a line is to have it bulk up on the reel and scrape on the reel bars. A little of this treatment and the line finish is finished.

There are three points to be kept in mind when purchasing a fly reel.

(1) It should be of sturdy construction, not subject to breakage from dropping or from any of the *average* fishing conditions it will be subjected to.

(2) It should fit snugly where the spool and shell meet, for if there is any space or ragged edges here, the line can easily get caught and will chafe at each revolution of the reel spool.

(3) It must be constructed for easy and quick takedown. This is necessary because when the reel is accidentally submerged in water, it must be dried. Also, all reels must be greased and oiled occasionally to assure smooth running and to safeguard against excessive wear of the moving parts.

Boots and Waders

The selection of proper wading gear is fully as important as the selection of your other tackle. Some years ago comfortable and adequate wading equipment was difficult to come by, but now the manufacturers have developed waders that are not only durable and waterproof but actually featherweight.

Some companies manufacture waders in three weights: heavy, medium and light. The heavyweight type offers years and years of wear but are bulky, heavy, and hot. The medium-weight waders will last several seasons with careful handling. The lightweight variety are very flexible and relatively cool, although care must be taken not to pull or snag them. The most modern development in waders is the new plastic stocking-foot light-weight ones you've probably seen at your tackle store. These are very handy in that they roll into a compact package and are wonderful for long overland treks, for you can wear your usual clothing and have them on in a jiffy. Certainly I hate to wear or carry heavy conventional-type waders on an overland hike.

All waders sweat from condensation due to the temperature difference between the inside and out. The fabric waders become damp to a much lesser degree, however, than the plastic variety, which do not breathe at all.

I've been talking exclusively of waders, but boots, too, have their advantages. Boots are much less cumbersome than most types of waders, are much cooler to wear in the summer months, and do not restrict the legs to the same degree as waders. The choice of waders or boots depends largely on the water you fish. If your streams are small and not too deep, boots will be adequate.

Waders that are too short or tight in the crotch will split open almost immediately. Waders that are too deep or loose in the crotch are even worse because they tend to constrict leg movement. When you buy waders or boots, try them on in the store. Ask the sales clerk for a pair of heavy socks, so that you will be sure you are getting the correct foot size, then test the crotch length. If it is necessary that you buy a size larger in the foot to accommodate the body fit, by all means do so, and figure on filling up the feet with another pair of socks. Put them on, complete with suspenders, bend your knees and kneel down with one knee on the floor. When you can do this, try one more test—stretch and see if you can touch your foot to the counter top easily. The wader that will do all this should enable you to fish with a minimum of restriction.

In buying wading shoes or brogues for stocking-foot waders, I prefer the lightest obtainable that will be strong. Make sure that they have lacing holes rather than buckles or hooks, for the latter can snag onto underwater obstructions and might cause you to trip or stumble. Wading brogues are expensive items but well worth the price in workmanship, leather, and lasting qualities. There are, however, several types of wading shoes, some part canvas and part rubber, which are certainly adequate for the purpose. The main thing to look for is a good sole which can be replaced easily and on which hobnails or felts can be secured.

There are a number of accessory slip-on and sandal arrangements which can be worn over ordinary boots or wader boot-bottoms. These are mighty handy if you want to change your boot-bottom aids to fit the existing circumstances. If, as an example, your shoes are felt-soled and you need chains or hobnails, it is a simple matter to put them on right over the felts. Chains are widely used and help in great measure to offer additional security. I carry accessory chains, felts, and hobnails in the back of the car to serve in any emergency. In general, felt soles are best for rocky bottoms, rubber soles for muddy bottoms. Chains or hob-nails are needed only for the slipperiest conditions.

Waders and boots can be made to last many seasons with a few precautions and simple care. Remember that both contain rubber, and rubber rots sooner or later. If you happen to be fishing a long time out of the water with the upper material exposed to the hot sun, sit down in the water occasionally to wet the fabric. If perchance your waders are wet inside from a spill or you want to dry them from internal sweat, do so in the shade. Turn them inside out for air circulation, and if excessive perspiration or con-densation is evident, wash them in a mild solution of castile soap and thoroughly rinse. Do this often, as the salt in perspiration rots rubber. When storing, hang by the feet in a brace that will hold the boot foot open. Place them in a relatively cool spot where they will not mildew. Never leave them where it is dry and warm.

When a scratch, tear, or worn spot develops be sure that the area is completely dry before attempting a patch. Periodic inspection is in order, and special attention must be paid to the seams. To make certain that your stock-ing-foot waders do not chafe or wear out quickly in the feet, be certain that all sand and grit is removed after each wearing. It pays to rinse out the shoes and remove sand that will have collected in them. Keep an eye on the felts and hobnails, and replace them before the wear reaches the leather part of the shoe. In short, if you give your wading equipment the same interest and care that you devote to your other tackle, you'll get your money's worth out of it. Fishing is a careful sport—or should be—but it need not be a prissy kind of operation. Certainly care of equipment goes hand in hand with careful wading, and this same quality applied to approach, presentation, and fishing strategy develops the successful angler.

Landing Nets

Virtually no piece of the angler's equipment receives as little care in selection or use as the landing net. Most anglers are constantly improving their tackle and will spend hours debating the tapers of rods and the types of lines, leaders and flies, yet they scarcely ever worry about their landing nets. They will study the various casts, perfect their approach, tie killing fly patterns but will go a-stream armed with the wrong net and be downright careless in its use. How many fish stories have you heard that end with the fish tearing loose just as it was about to be landed or being safely in the net only to flop out or, worse still, slip through a hole in the meshes?

In the stream-landing-net department there are inexpensive small wire-hoop and wood-handled jobs that are capable of holding trout up to, say, ten inches. These nets can be used and carried with ease because of their size. Their big drawback comes when you hook into a really sizable fish and are armed with the tea-cup type when you should have a veritable barrel.

The most practical hoop dimensions for everything but steelhead and salmon fishing should be about twenty inches from stem to bottom of the hoop bend and at least fifteen inches across, preferably more. I also prefer an almost triangular shape rather than one too round, because then I can feel free to scuff the gravel with the flat bottom of the hoop when necessary, to make sure the fish doesn't make a dash under the net.

Some anglers like those infernal elastic-corded nets which inevitably snag on a bush, stretch to the limit and then snap into your back like the hoof of a mad deer! These can, however, be hung to avoid this, and the elastic comes in handy for stretching the net out to reach a trout. Other nets come with a quickly detachable cord, but I have seen more than one net lost in the current, left after lunch on the bank, or in some cases, dropped from the hand in the frantic moment of bringing the monster in. You can't have everything, and the man who solves all the net-design problems will have that better mousetrap!

The mesh size of the net bag is not too important a consideration, as most of those available commercially are about the same. I prefer those which have a graduated web smaller at the bottom because, in the event a few of the strands become broken, the fish will not be so likely to escape. My own hand-made landing net has a special small web for use in catching nymphs and minnows, and it comes in mighty handy. It has its drawbacks, too, however—the water doesn't flow through it fast enough.

Beware of the stringy-type cotton bags. They will break easily when snagged, will not last more than a season, and will not stand up under the tear of bass fins or the spines and scales of some game fish. Look for net bags made of stout material, specially treated, or in the case of nylon, strongly and tightly woven. Make certain that the junction with the net hoop is secure. Smart net manufacturers don't put a sleazy net bag on a good hoop. In any case, make certain that the net bag can easily be replaced.

If a net with a detachable loop cord is used and if boots and creel are part of the basic equipment, the net cord goes around my waist with the snap end being slipped between my belt and pants. It hangs from the left side, as I prefer the creel to rest under my right casting arm. When I have to walk through the woods or brush I detach the net and carry it along with my rod broken down, in my right hand. Upon netting a fish, I either detach it or stretch the net out as far as necessary. When wearing waders and a jacket with a built-in creel or rubber game pocket, I place the elastic cord over the right shoulder with the net slung under the left armpit. When going through heavy brush, as an extra precaution I slip the net in the waders or put it partially under my jacket.

A single-strand net cord with a snap-on end can be attached most effectively to the wader suspenders or the ring in the creel harness. Depending on the amount of heavy clothes you are wearing, you can hook the net catch onto a belt or snap it onto a jacket loop so that it's out of the way and doesn't interfere with walking or, more important, doesn't tangle with the slack line while fishing.

If you possess one of the collapsible landing nets that snap into action at the flip of the wrist, the place to attach it is on the special ring and loop found on some wading jackets. The staunch cloth loop, attached at the top of the collar in the center of the back neck edge, is about seven inches long and holds a ring. Attach the end of the net cord and the net handle clamp to the ring. With the net folded, sling the works over your left shoulder if you are a right-handed caster. When you want the net, simply dip the left shoulder and it will flop over onto your chest and in one second the net handle is detached from the ring and in another second the net hoop is snapped open for action.

CHAPTER II
Fishing the Wet Fly

General Theory

From time immemorial, the trout has been glorified by anglers—his colors, his form, his power, and his ability to detect the most carefully made artificial. When hooked, his determination to shake himself free is extraordinary. The trout that escapes is much larger in the angler's mind than those reposing in the creel.

Many legendary trout have been credited with extraordinary caginess, and there is scarcely a brook or stream that does not harbor an "Old Ragged Fin." This is always a fish of gigantic proportions, usually living in a hole or under a bridge and no matter how many anglers try for it, their efforts go for naught.

These attributed qualities of perception and brain power on the part of the trout are to my mind wonderful bits of anglers' imaginings, designed to excuse an empty creel. It is not so much that trout are intelligent; rather it is a matter of the fishermen not being as much so as they suppose. Actually, the trout has few secrets. He has but three prime worries in life: filling his stomach, keeping out of danger, and carrying on his species. To accomplish these three duties, he has been endowed by nature with excellent eyesight, the ability to move fast, and the power to migrate long distances. Biologists say that the trout has a one-track mind, so it would seem that catching him would be a very simple matter. But fortunately for the trout, there are many complex elements in his environment which present obstacles to the angler. These complexities do not lie in the fish's brain but, rather, in the mystery of the current.

During the angling season the weather, water height, temperature, and degree of light greatly affect the trout and his feeding habits. In the early season the temperature of the stream rises during the middle of the day, causing the nymphs to hatch and the fish to feed. The water is cold in the morning hours, and neither the insects nor the trout will be active to any degree.

Later in the year the stream is lower and warmer, and the insects hatch in the fast-moving stretches either in the late afternoon or early evening, for they wait until the high midday temperature has dropped. It is then that the trout also venture forth to feed under cover of the shadows.

The summer season finds most of the hatches occurring at dusk or nightfall, and here again the cooler temperatures bring forth the trout activity.

The alert angler can discover the many streamside guides which point to the particular lure and type of angling required at the moment. Important fishing lessons can also be learned by watching others. To watch a successful angler is to gain a store of knowledge. Relatively few anglers take their sport seriously enough to indulge in observation of the stream, but those who do are the ten per cent who will catch ninety per cent of the fish—the men who return most, if not all, of the fish they catch. To reach this point is to my mind the ultimate, the top rung of the ladder.

The attitude among elite dry-fly men that wet-fly fishing is only "chuck and chance it" gets no quarter in these pages. Wet-fly and dry-fly schools are but overlapping forms leading to the complete whole of fly fishing. They should never be considered as separate entities. It has been said that wet-fly fishing is the ideal method for the beginner. The basics of wet-fly casting are easy for the beginner to master, true, but to *catch fish* with the wet fly is, in my opinion, no easier than it is with any other method of fishing. As a matter of fact, I have helped many people to cast and have invariably started them with the dry fly, for it is much easier for them to see their cast on the water, recognize their mistakes in delivery, and control slack or drag when either develops. The beginner is fascinated by the floating fly. There is the added chance that even without sophisticated handling, the floater will take a small fish, and, believe me, there is nothing so reassuring to pupil as well as to teacher as a hooked fish, even if the fish be small.

Potency of the Wet Fly

One cold blustery day a wet fly securely tied to a fine leader is cast well across the midstream current. In a matter of seconds the fly sinks, dragged under by the force of the water. Down, down it goes, whisking by rocks and snags to pause momentarily over the gravel behind a big rock. A trout is resting there—a large one. The fly moves upward with the hackles undulating in a lifelike manner. The shadow of the trout glides near and just as the fly is about to be drawn from the pocket he lunges for it with deadly accuracy and takes it in his mouth.

The wet fly may imitate a nymph, a water insect, a small minnow, or almost anything that resembles food. Its coloration and general appearance fit into nearly any angling situation, making it truly the most universal of all lures in fly-fishing.

Time and again I have marveled at the "luck" that has come my way when using my sparsely dressed No. 16's. One of my favorites for New York's Westchester streams is a pattern I've dubbed the Commuter Special, for it is effective within fifty miles of New York City, especially on the many watershed streams. These waters yield fabulous fish to the few metropolitan anglers who work them with persistent care and caution. These fish live in better-than-average circumstances. They have clear cold water throughout the season, an advantage not always found in "natural" streams. Most of this water is in the form of connecting links between the huge reservoirs, and it is constantly full of feed. The fly life is mostly small caddis flies, stone flies and mayflies, and during the months of April and May the shady conditions affect the dark-brown and black colorations on the insects. My "Commuter" is so designed, tied sparse. The two tail fibers are black-brown and stiff. The body is of black-brown quill over black tying thread with grizzly hackle and mallard wings, and it is a combination that has consistently outfished many of the "standards."

In the discussion of wet-fly fishing technique, several questions always pop up. When is the fly near the fish? Can it be determined whether the fish are feeding underwater if they cannot actually be seen in the act? Is the lure moving naturally? Is it the right size and pattern? These and many more questions arise, especially when we have been on the water for a considerable time fishing hard but receiving no results from our efforts. Many of us go fishing year after year without attempting to find the answers, or at least some theoretical conclusions which can be catalogued for future use.

In this circumstance, any fish taken are really "luck." We are in reality searching the water with the fly for a trout that will come up and take it. There is nothing wrong with this method (no method of fishing is ever "wrong" if it is enjoyable, results or not). The "chuck and chance it" method is sometimes the only one which will pay off. There are times when all theories break down, and as the last resort the angler keeps on fishing, of course varying his techniques occasionally and changing flies often until a fish is caught. But when a plan of attack is mapped out and fish are taken in view of anglers having fewer or no results in the same water, it is generally not luck in the "accident" sense of the word. It is likely to be the result of knowledge and application. One feels "lucky" when the fruits of observation pay off.

Patterns and Types

Wet-fly patterns fall into two classifications: those that are an attempt at exact imitation and those which are called attractor types for the want of better terminology. These last-mentioned are mainly the outcome of the fly tier's creative artistry. There are countless thousands of them, and any one of them will catch fish at some time or other if fished long and hard enough.

The wet-flies that are an attempt at close imitation are the somber and drab combinations of fur and feather which simulate the general appearance of numerous insect types found in and along the stream. A few basic patterns have proven deadly as steady fish getters on all streams at all seasons of the year.

Results can be had with the Leadwing Coachman from opening day to the last trout of the year, yet I know this fly cannot appear to the trout as an exact imitation of anything. Whether its allure is the lead-colored wings that resemble the back of a nymph or the wings of a dead adult fly is open to question. Perhaps the appeal lies in the peacock herl that simulates the body and gills of a nymph.

Another wet fly that I am very partial to is the Hare's Ear, either gold ribbed or with fluffed-up body. The gold-ribbed pattern is especially good during the opening of the season. When fished deep in roily water it is mistaken by the trout for the nymphal form of many of the smaller mayflies, caddis flies, and stone flies.

A third stand-by is the Cahill, either light or dark. This fly with the barred wings should be tied sparse to resemble a rising nymph, with the hackle and wings lying almost straight back on the hook shank.

The Gray or Brown Hackle, two of the most famous of all trout flies, should be in every trout angler's box. Hackle flies are very good nymph and "bug" imitations when tied with webby hackle to resemble insects' legs.

If I could have only these four wet flies in sizes from 8 to 16, they would serve me well. The more I fish, the more it becomes obvious to me that I have paid entirely too much attention to pattern and not enough to actual fishing. A wet fly fished over barren water, or with the wrong presentation, will attract only the occasional "accidental" trout. The angler who can "read" the stream and goes out equipped with the proper rig can catch his share of trout with almost any pattern.

There are many reasons why trout are often found in some places and hardly ever in others. Where the current becomes strong, trout must swim too hard to stay in location. Naturally they cannot swim against the current continuously without becoming exhausted. It is true that fish are taken from water flowing very fast—*on the surface*. Underneath the white stuff, there are holes before and behind rocks, ledges and snags where the water is not so swift, and here is where the trout lie. Where the stream bed is flat and made up of sand and small gravel the stream current is practically the same down deep as it is up above. Place some big stones or boulders in there and the water on the bottom would be deflected and slowed.

Temperatures are all-important. At 42 degrees, a trout's digestion process takes about five days. At 52 degrees the time is about twenty-four hours. The shortest digestion period appears to take place at about 66 degrees. When the temperature goes up to 70 or more, little feeding is done. The deductions from this are a constant on which we can depend. Fish eat less in very cold or very warm water. To feed in comfort, they head for the more agreeable temperatures, or wait for them to occur (warmer during the day if the weather is cold, or cooler at night when the daytime is hot).

Light enters the picture too. Trout like the shadows, and so do many of the stream-bred insects. In the summer or on bright days the fish will be under cover, which may be in the fast water or in holes and pockets. They might feed in an entirely different location than their resting place.

One May day I spent more than an hour working over a particular trout that I had noticed feeding at the head of a pool. For a long time I cast to him from above, drifting a couple of wet flies, but evidently there was something wrong, for he stopped feeding. Either I had scared him or the downstream presentation of the conventional wet-fly rig was unnatural enough to interrupt his activity.

I went ashore and watched the water for a few minutes, trying to think of a new approach and to await his feeding. In about ten minutes he reappeared, timidly at first, and gradually began to fan the current, occasionally picking up stray nymphs that were drifting down to him from above.

With a fresh approach in mind, I waded in at the tail of
the pool to fish up to him. The first cast fell near and hardly
had it hit the water when I felt a quick pull followed by a
sudden dash. Automatically I raised the rod tip but sensed
immediately that it was not the big fellow that I had taken.
I brought the little trout out of the area as quickly as
possible with a minimum of disturbance and recast well
above where the trout had last shown. I mentally followed
the course my fly would take and as it drew close to him I
tensed my wrist for the strike. The fly drifted well below
and as I raised the rod for a recast another trout hit, and
there was action with a snappy little rainbow.

My big trout was still heaving porpoiselike on the surface
and the very sight of him sent shivers up my spine. Cau-
tiously moving upstream, I again cast above and hoped
that this cast would do the trick. The fly passed his very
nose, and suddenly the line straightened. I struck hard. It
was a grand battle, and the trout went through his book of
tricks: thrashing the surface, sounding the depths, and
taking to both sides of the pool in search of a snag. He shone
brightly as I brought him to the net and to my mind was
one of the most beautifully marked, well-shaped fish I have
ever had the fortune to hook. Best of all, I had discovered
that in a case like this, one fly well delivered was all that
was needed. Unfortunately, I bungled the last stage of the
fight by careless use of the net and lost one of the best fish
I've ever hooked. It's a good idea to wait until your fish is
safely landed before you begin to admire your catch.

Two or Three Wet Flies

Two wet flies are usually ample when working across and
down the fast stretches of a stream where the current is
broken, for the leader connections will be less obvious to

the fish due to the refraction of light by the churning water surface. A brightly colored dropper attached well up from the tail fly serves both as a guide to following the cast in the water and as an attractor for the tail fly, which more resembles something to eat. There is no question that this arrangement offers more than one inducement. The current carries them downstream, and as they swing wide they are retrieved in short, snappy twitches.

Three flies are effective in wilderness waters, especially for brook trout. It is easy to discover the trout's preference when two or three flies are offered. If, for instance, a dark fly is on the end, a medium-colored one in the middle, and a bright or light one on top, it can quickly be determined what type of fly is being taken.

A Vermont friend invited me to fish with him and rigged my leader with a White Miller on top, a little March Brown in the middle, and a Black Gnat on the tippet. After watching his first few casts, I mimicked his style of letting the current swing the flies in an arc across the water and into the side pockets among the rocks. In quick succession we hooked four brookies, and both of us discovered that they had taken the middle fly.

"That's why I like to fish with three flies," he said. "It is three times easier to find out what they are taking."

Observation Pays Off

I'll never forget the big brown on Mills Pool, for the experience taught me the wonderful advantage and absolute necessity of careful observation, approach, and presentation.

I had never been so mad at the world. Through sheer clumsiness I'd broken the tip of my best rod. It was bad enough to have broken it, but to make matters worse, it

meant that I had to forgo the chance of taking a big brown that I had been working over for some days, and recently for a period of an hour. He was just in the mood to strike; I had seen him move several times. I was certain that he would have taken my next cast.

I sat dejectedly on an old log, gloomily staring at my scowling reflection. Just out there in the current the brownie occasionally changed position to take bits of food borne down the pool. As I watched intently, anger turned to interest, for here was the opportunity to observe a summer trout and his actions.

Though feeding time had long passed, the brown was not averse to sucking a nymph down below or rising to the surface if a particularly succulent insect floated by. I noted several lesser trout in the same general run, but because of his size this brownie was more distinguishable.

His lair was a big deep pool headed by a series of water-falls and sluices and tailed by a gradually shallowing pointed rapids. The current in the body of the pool was S-shaped, and the smaller trout were nosing into the upper curve, while my brown remained contentedly in about five feet of water in the lower belly of the current.

I studied him for some time, wondering at the amount of free ranging he was doing from surface to bottom, while rarely straying sideways from the current stretch. He eyed each bit of food carefully, and after gliding to it, drifted back to his former position and swallowed his prey. Among other things, I learned that it is not always the choice of lure that takes fish, for here was a perfect example of a trout that semed to sample everything, though he was not actually on a feeding spree. He took these insects because they drifted by him *naturally*.

I was about to abandon my study of the brownie when I spied an angler working his way up toward the pool and decided to wait and see if he would take the fish.

Soon the newcomer was laying out a neat line with beautiful rod execution, a delight to watch. He was using a fly which appeared to be of the Ginger Quill type, a close copy of those few naturals that were on the water, but the only effect on the brownie was to cause him to move down toward the bottom and fan the water uneasily.

The angler covered the pool well, never once making a sloppy cast or allowing any visible drag, nor did he retrieve the fly from the water with the slightest disturbance. He did, however, overlook one very important point that sometimes is the deciding factor in fisherman's "luck." He neglected to analyze the current in relation to any trout that might be there. Had he taken a few minutes to observe the water before casting and ascertained the spots where it would be reasonable that fish would lie, then directed his position and casting angle accordingly, he would have connected with at least one of the smaller trout and possibly would have interested the big one. Chances are that he retired from the stream with the usual excuse that the fish were not feeding that day.

The next morning, I went back to the pool armed with the spare rod tip and luckily found that conditions were exactly the same as they were the day before, a rarity in trout angling. The light was the same, the brownie still there and feeding lazily. I waded in at the tail of the S current where the rapids would cover my approach. The fly was cast to the head of the pool and drifted down into the body of the S, directly into the brownie's path of vision. Taking him that day should have been like taking candy from a baby. Some days nothing will work.

Another incident proved this business of planning through observation. For many years I had fished one particular pool on a favorite river with success, yet I knew there were bigger fish there than I could take from that potent water. The pool is a large and long one. The bank on the side I had never fished was steep, rock-strewn, and brushy. Quite naturally, I had avoided that side and been content to heave long casts to the deep and broken water skirting this forbidding bank. The manipulation of the nymph was all but impossible when working from the usual side. Despite this I had taken good fish in this manner, but as I said before, the bigger ones were still in there.

One afternoon, the sight of big rainbows and browns rising freely just beyond casting distance helped make up my mind to give that water a whirl from the other bank. Over I went to the forbidding rocks and brambles and finally reached the water in an area that was wadeable just above the location of the largest of the rising fish. Every few minutes one of the big boys came up to rush at a passing nymph, and I knew that I'd have to fish carefully despite the confusion of the fast water surface. While teetering on a precarious footing and trying to stay upright in the fast current I was finally able to roll cast several times in front of the fish. The effort paid off and I returned that evening with three nice trout ... bigger ones than I have taken in that pool before or since.

Toward the end of that same season, our stream was almost bare. The magnificent river was but a shadow of its former self. Disconsolate over the conditions, Ernie and I were sitting on the front porch of the club, Ernie busying himself with a crossword puzzle.

"Say, Ernie, we are missing a wonderful opportunity."

"Uh," he said, not taking his eyes off the paper. "What's a word for 'feline'? Three letters, middle one's *a*."

"Let's take a walk down to the stream and dry run some of these holes and riffles. Maybe we can learn something," I returned.

Briefly, that afternoon and for three days, we walked up and down the dry bed of the river, recalling fishing problems that had puzzled us. We took up familiar casting positions and viewed runs that had appeared fast during normal water height, but now revealed a broken bottom that afforded generous resting spots for the fish to lie and hold in.

The following season we fished this water together, and the hours of observation we had spent during the dry spell paid off generously in future days of fishing rare indeed in this angler's experience.

There are many ways in which observation pays off. Have you ever watched an angler who is catching fish and asked him what fly or technique was doing the trick? Have you ever walked along a stream and made an informal survey of rod lengths, rod materials, leader lengths, fly patterns, and so forth? Another source of information is the tackle store. Find out what lures are selling best. Ask questions wherever you go. Keep your eyes open when on the stream and pay attention to the techniques of others. You'll end up with a great deal of what might be called unmeasurable evidence. For example, three anglers fishing wet flies all took trout, each using a different pattern. The question then reverts to presentation. How did they present their flies—on the surface or deep, worked or dead drift? Were they fishing two flies at a time? What sizes did they use? Consistent success results from constant observation and questioning.

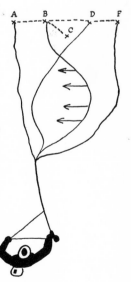

MENDING THE CAST

One way of presenting the fly to the fish without the interference of a dragging line is by simply raising the rod tip and, without moving the leader, flipping the line upstream in the motion of a modified roll cast. It is sometimes necessary to do this two or three times during a drift, especially when the current is moving fast between you and the fly. This is called "mending the cast."

STOP CAST

In direct downstream fishing the stop cast is sometimes employed. False cast in the downstream direction, but on the forward swing of the line check the rod at the vertical. The line will belly forward in the air but the fly will drop into the water a few feet below your position. Control the slack of the cast by bringing the rod tip back and then ease it forward as the lure drifts downstream. When fishing pocket water retrieve in a zigzag pattern.

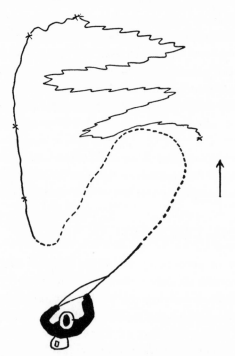

Diagram of the downstream stop cast

Dotted line shows the line in the air after the forward throw is stopped. The line and fly have landed almost under the rod and will drift naturally in the current and will sink.

The zigzag retrieve is shown to demonstrate complete water coverage.

This simulates the escaping form of life or hatching insect.

WORKING THE FLY

There are countless ways of handling the wet fly to make it appear natural to the trout. Most of these are variations of the two extremes of presentation—"dead drift" and "escaping form."

The dead-drift fly has no imparted action given to it by the angler nor is it allowed to have any unnatural drag from

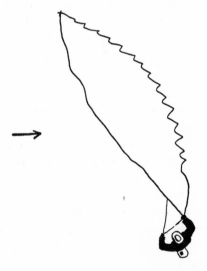

Diagram of the conventional across-stream cast
and quick retrieve

the action of the current on the line. The "escaping form" is the extreme opposite in that the lure is activated by the angler in combination with current drag to imitate active underwater insect life.

DEAD-DRIFT FLY

This method is used effectively in the main feeding lanes during the times when there is no apparent feeding activity by the trout. It is a good early-season technique, for in cold weather the fish are not usually prone to chase after active flies and will often take the slower-moving morsel when it comes near them. High and fast water will dislodge many of the insects, leaving them to drift along at the will of the current. One excellent pattern is the imitation of the green caddis worm, in streams where this insect is prevalent. Another is the March Brown and the Gold Ribbed Hare's Ear, for they double well for the mayfly and stone fly nymphs that are abundant on the stream bottom and in and around the pockets and holes in the main current.

Later in the season the dead-drift style imitates the gradual downstream movement of many of the insects still in their partially developed nymphal stage. In the height of the season, usually after a hatch, the wet fly that is dead drifted near the surface imitates the spent aquatic insects and also those countless varieties of land-bred insects that have found their way to the water and drowned. In all instances, the dead-drift style of fishing should be employed in moving water, especially in places where the current tends to concentrate into a run. The spots where food and stream refuse are seen in abundance are the places to dead drift the artificial.

The dead drift is very similar in execution to dry-fly fishing and requires an equal amount of finesse. Avoiding any unnatural drag to the fly is a difficult feat in this type of fishing. Any drag will tend to pull the lure or make it move unnaturally. It is, I admit, a pretty problem to cast so that the leader will lie upstream from the fly. In wet-fly fishing when the water is high and heavy, it is as important to pay particular attention to the drag and position of the leader as it is in dry-fly fishing.

In fishing the dead-drift method, a position is taken slightly below the point where the lure will be fished. Cast it

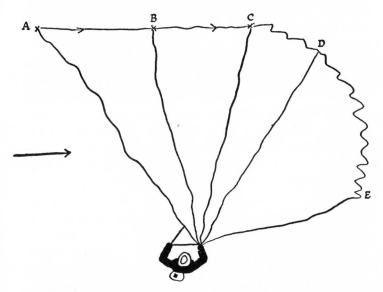

Diagram of combined "dead drift" and across-stream "escaping form" retrieve

Note that the first part of the drift (A to B) is drag free with no slack line, allowing the fly to sink in the water (C). The across-stream retrieve is then used to work over the selected area, and the fly is taken from the water only when it is well out of the fishing area (D).

at least twenty to thirty feet above in the lane of the current, much in the manner of dry-fly fishing, so that the lure will sink well into the eddies. The further upstream the fly is cast, the more opportunity it has to sink. By guiding the slack line with the rod tip, you can make the lure follow along its course naturally and out below the area on which you are concentrating. It is very important to fish out the cast to the very end and, if possible with careful working, to cast and recast several times in a given area, experimenting with various depths, yet still not scare the fish. A typical situation is found in many mountain streams. The waterfalls cascade over big boulders and into big pools which usually shallow out near the end in obvious channels. A close look at these lanes will reveal holes and boulders, holding water for the biggest fish in the stretch. A little preplanning will save time and energy, for it is almost always possible to work these hot spots from quite a distance, and after solving the problems presented by these types of water, the angler can analyze the stream with cold perception like that of a billiard player sizing up a scoring angle shot.

ESCAPING FORM OF LIFE

The action of the lure makes this type of presentation attractive to the trout, for when using this technique we attempt to imitate an active nymph or stream insect and in some instances small minnows or trout fry. This fishing style is fairly easy for the beginner to master. The lure is manipulated with the rod tip to simulate self-propelled movement. It is particularly killing in quiet or semiquiet water where the erratic action would be most noticeable to the trout.

A fly is cast across to the head of the run and guided past the rocks and snags with a twitching motion of the rod tip and an occasional mending side cast. When the imitation reaches a back current or deep open spot, permit it to sink and then swim erratically back and forth across the area, again letting out a little slack line. After retrieving the lure from pocket to pocket in short minnowlike jerks and twitches, repeat the process and again let it fall downstream. Take the fly from the water well away from a spot that is at all fishable, for any sudden unnatural action, such as a long length of line cutting up the surface on retrieve, will cause even the boldest of the big trout to scurry away.

Many times when I have been resting on the stream bank I have observed other anglers as they fished a stretch of water. I can recall many instances when I have seen trout flash and dart away as a result of too much casting and sloppy line retrieve. It pays to watch the other fellow!

WASHINGTON STATE CUTTHROAT

While stationed at Fort Lewis, Washington, during the Second War, I had a full year of basic training in both salmon and trout angling, particularly cutthroat-trout fishing, as so much of it was available within a short distance of the Fort.

These trout seem to react better to the wet fly than to the dry. It was hardly ever that twenty-five or thirty of these trout could not be taken and released during an afternoon, when they could be taken at all.

I fished for them in the nearby lakes and the streams draining from Mount Ranier. I also worked the Olympic Peninsula lakes and streams. The Skokumchuck River offered my first exciting experience in cutthroat angling.

The day we left Fort Lewis on this excursion it was raining—a typical, very wet Washington rain. Hasty handshakes amid an unwanted downpour introduced us to our hosts at the little outpost town of Vail. Driving rain pelted against the windows of the logging train that was to carry us to some of the best fishing this writer has ever seen.

During our bumpy ride the rain ceased long enough to offer a colorful glimpse of Mount Rainier. The sun spotted the majestic beauty of the glacier cushioned in mist and bathed in pink radiance. Everything below was in the twilight glow of tinted fog, rain, and wet—magnificent in its sogginess.

I was unable to sleep that night. I never can on the eve of opening day, and this one in particular was an occasion. I lay awake, listening to the rain on the roof, dreaming of the thrills ahead, figuring in advance the tackle and flies I'd use—and hoping for a letup in the weather. The rain persisted throughout the night, and several times I snapped on my flashlight to check the time. Fred Jennings of Olympia, Washington, tossed and turned in his bunk. He too was anxious.

The damp of dawn brought shivers, and after a sample of the frigid deluge I decided to light the fire and dish up eggs and bacon and plenty of good black coffee. Starting right on a morning like this was a good idea. After sampling this potent brew, none would have known whether it was raining or not.

Fred caught the first fish and returned him safely to the water—a superb trout of five inches!

"Give him your telephone number," I yelled, "and tell him to look you up in a few years. Where are those big cutthroats you've been telling me about?"

"Right here," he answered on cue as his rod bent in a shimmering arc. "He isn't big, but he's one to warm up on."

"What kind of fly is causing all this action?" I asked when we got under a windfall to dump the water out of our hatbrims. At this point, driving rain came crashing down the canyon in an unbelievable downpour, shelving all thoughts of fly-fishing. We lit cigarettes and surveyed the rain-spattered surface of the pool ahead. Finally, Fred reached for his bottle of salmon eggs, produced some tiny hooks and without looking up started to tie one on the leader where he had just snipped off a fly. A couple of purists then yielded to bait!

This turned the tide of luck. The sun began to break through in spots, making it warmer and easier going. Scant patches of blue sky cheered our drenched spirits and dried out the overhanging foliage. It was fun to cast alongside the huge rocks, fallen timber, and burned-over windfalls—the ancient charred ruins of a forest primeval.

Our shoulders dried out little by little, and the warm sun shone brightly down into the water, revealing slender cutthroats. It would make your heart pump through your ribs to see those big graceful beauties avoid our offerings. It looked easy, but the most response we'd elicit was a casual flip of a fin. Then the general movement of the group would settle down to the rhythmic fanning of the caudals and the clocklike opening and closing of the gills.

I turned at a yelp from Fred to see the water exploding under his arched rod that shivered like a man in his early morning shower. The line slit the surface, and a big cutthroat leaped salmonlike into the air, plainly showing his spots and his broad burnished side. On the other end of the tackle Fred was pretty excited. His brow knitted when I reminded him that his terminal tackle wouldn't stand too much. He led the fish toward the shore, when with a burst of lunges that raised the hair on the back of my neck, this mountain trout reached out for the safety of the deep. I crossed the pool via the rapids below to help with the eventual netting. After minutes of breath-taking action, Fred brought the fish in close, and it quite accidentally dove into my submerged net. Together we measured the trout's nineteen inches of gallant length, a true fighter born of mountain heritage and the unbounded strength of the sea.

We caught many good fish that day on small Silver Doctor patterns fished deep and worked fast and erratically, but the climax of the trip for me came when the sun had fallen into the shadows and, typical of the Washington springtime, the pinks, reds, and purples of the clouds were ever changing against the blue-green of the Northwest sky. What a glorious afternoon!

I was forewarned of the big trout to come as I saw the snout of the whopper rise up and suck a fly from the surface. I found the insect he was taking—comparable to a Blue Dun tied back East in a Maine tackle store. The cast straightened out in the air and the Dun settled beautifully. There was a sudden and powerful jab. This fellow meant business. When his intended feast turned out to be only feathers and a hook, he showed an enraged eye. Cutthroats, I was finding out this twilight, were not to be trifled with.

I yelled for Fred, but he was beyond sight and hearing. I was to settle this account without moral assistance. After staving off run after run and jump after jump, I directed the final round from the shore to avoid any dashes downstream and perhaps the loss of a fine fish. The shadows were long and deep when the battle let up. The trout swam in under the rod for the last of a long series of threats. He measured two lengths of my creel ruler, a fine specimen of a Washington cutthroat from one of the wildest, coldest streams in our Northwest.

These western trout seem to go for the bright and shiny

fly patterns, and gold or silver trim seems to be a fly requisite even in the water-clear water of the mountain streams. Despite the fact that these fish are similar in type and habit to the rainbow, they prefer an active wet fly over a slow or dead-drift presentation. They also resemble closely the striking and fighting of the eastern brook trout.

The "active fly" method is especially productive in morning and twilight fishing for brook trout in the northern streams. These trout seem to be attracted by the motion of the fly more often than they are by a fly that is drifted naturally. When conditions are right and the killing pattern is found, it is not at all uncommon to hook two fish at once on a two- or three-fly leader, if a fast retrieve is used. Only on few occasions have I found this technique of much use in the slower sections of Catskill waters when brown trout are the quarry. Occasionally a big rainbow can be lured from his pocket behind a big boulder with this method, but when the water is clear and low, I use this system as a last resort before moving on to the next position downstream.

POPPING THE FLY

In quiet water it is often advisable to offer a bit of motion in order to attract the attention of the trout. When such duns as the Hendricksons and the March Browns have just emerged, they sometimes flex their wings and perhaps hop about on the surface. This action can be duplicated in slow water, about the only place where it would be noticed by the trout. Have your rod in a vertical position and give a short but quick snap of the rod tip, lowering it to the water, which will give it slack line and so eliminate drag.

I have found this little trick quite effective in general quiet-water angling. It is called for when insects are seen

floating on the surface but no action by the trout is visible. The sight of the wriggling insects arouses even the logy ones, and I believe it brings out in them the instinct of the chase. It can be compared with the cat and the wounded mouse.

ADD A BOBBER FLY

A bobber fly can be added to the butt of a leader to act as a guide. I came upon this idea while fishing the upper reaches of the Rio Grande in New Mexico.

At the tail of a riffle I spotted a sizable brown nosing the bottom. He was out in the open in plain sight, and realizing that I would have few chances before he would scare into deeper water, I promptly tied a dry fly on a dropper near the top of a leader and a wet of the same pattern on the tapered end. The cast fell well above in clear water about two feet deep. I reasoned that the dry fly might draw his attention and he would then have a choice of the two. Using the dry fly as a guide to the position of the wet, I gradually worked the line across, keeping the wet fly trailing behind about a foot beneath the surface. All of a sudden the big fish turned toward the dry fly, paused, saw the wet imitation and lunged for it. I set the hook the moment I felt the smashing take.

SKITTERING

Another technique of fishing with a bobber fly is that of skittering it along the surface while the wet fly travels underneath. The commotion of the skittered fly arouses the trout, and seeing both he can grab at one or the other, though usually you will find that the sunken fly will win out.

Skittering the fly is just a bolder method of the popping style of presentation. This can be used effectively in almost any type of water and is particularly effective during a hatch of fast-water flies. Here drag is used to great advantage, so capitalize on it. Many of the mayflies skitter and hop over the water in an effort to take off into the air. Here again the chase instinct is brought forth. Many is the time I have seen trout take these active flies and let others float by unmolested. When there is a breeze and some of the flies are knocked to the surface this skittering technique with the wet fly fished with a greased leader can be very killing.

Evening is one of the best times to employ the skittering technique with a spider fly. When the spinners are returning to lay their eggs on the water, they seem to skitter on the surface, take off again and return. This action is what makes the trout lose all caution. Employ the drag to advantage and skitter the spider fly, casting and recasting over the same area.

MIDGE FISHING

I debated for a long time before inserting this bit of angling experience because, first of all, many of the angling clan consider midge fishing as dry-fly fishing. Nevertheless, I beg to invade the territory, since my experience in fishing with tiny No. 18 and 20 flies has been largely subsurface.

Though I would never recommend midge fishing to the beginner, I have come to rely on these small flies for hard-to-catch trout under certain conditions. For one thing, it takes time to build up much confidence in such small flies. Only "luck" will develop that confidence, and the indiscriminate use of them will discourage the most courageous. Like many types of flies, midges, black-fly larvae imitations, or whatever you choose to call them, are extremely difficult to present properly. They are most often taken just under the surface film or inches below in moving currents. They are only effective when the trout are feeding on the naturals. Thus exposed so near the surface, trout are extremely cautious and selective. The only reason they will feed on these tiny naturals is that they are present in huge quantities. Under this condition the imitation has no particular individual attraction. It is only one of many that the trout will take into his mouth as he cruises along.

The line and part of the leader must be greased well to float, but the last four feet of it must be extremely fine and grease-free. This sort of a rig is difficult to cast, and perfect, noiseless delivery is a must. The line and leader must never cause an unnatural action of the lure. Too much slack will be responsible for lost strikes; too tight a line will tend to pull the fly from the fish's mouth, for he "drinks" or "sucks" in the fly; he does not strike it.

Despite all these facts, midge fishing is an unforgettable fishing experience when graced with hits and a good-sized trout in the creel. After you have taken your first twenty-inch rainbow on a size-20 fly on 6X nylon in broken water, with a gallery watching—brother, you are elected to the "expert" class.

It is most difficult to obtain well-tied flies on size-20 hooks. In tying midges, I generally confine myself to three patterns—black, dark brown, and gray or grizzly. Tie in only three short thin hackle fibers, use tying silk for a very short and thin body, and use only two turns of the smallest hackle points from a hackle neck.

For experimental purposes fish three of these flies, each of a different coloration on the same leader, on short tippets, all grouped in the thin-end section of the leader. Cast it with care, for when this rig becomes tangled, it is exasperating to work on, especially when the trout are feeding in front of your nose. The rise does not last long, so get in as many casts as possible before it is all over.

Midge fishing is usually productive early in the season or sometimes during the "dead spots" in May and June when the mayfly hatches are sporadic. One of the best times is on a May evening when the black flies you are tying to represent are going to work on you. Signs of midge feeding are obvious. The trout only dimple and will, on occasion, show their tails and fins.

Obviously, size-20 hooks must be sharp and well tied to the leader. The strike cannot be hard and should only be a gradual tightening as the fish turns and is felt. When a trout is hooked in this way it will invariably be found that the hook is well embedded in the mouth or at the base of the tongue, or even further down. A sudden hard strike will snap the tippet, straighten out the light wire, or cause the leader to rough up against the fish's teeth. Believe me, when you have mastered the art of hooking, playing, and landing fish with any consistency with these small flies you'll have added one more pleasure to your angling.

Any fisherman who spends a reasonable amount of time on the stream has at some time or other come up against the brain-addling problem of midge-feeding trout. The familiar picture is something like this. The pool is usually quite calm, we cannot see any insects on the surface or in the air, and the trout are steadily "humping" the water as they suck in some mysterious food particle. Our old standby dry flies do not seem to interest even the smallest trout, and the punkies are having a smörgasbord on the backs of our necks. No, I don't have the answer to all of these problems, but if you are interested, here are a few ideas that have worked for me when the problem of the invisible hatch has presented itself.

First of all, get as close as possible to the feeding fish. You can present your fly much more delicately from fifteen feet · than you can from forty feet. Trout that are feeding on small insects seem to keep their attention focused on their business and are not nearly as shy then as they are at other times. But the casting must be done with a minimum of surface disturbance, or the trout will recognize your offering at once for what it is—a phony.

After you are in position to cast to your fish, try to determine if the food he is taking is on, under, or *in* the surface of the water. This is half the battle, and once this is decided the rest is *almost* easy. If the insect is on the surface, you should be able to see it by lowering your face to within twelve inches of the water. It is sometimes amazing the abundance of surface food one can see from this position. If you increase the distance between your eye and the water to a yard or more, this same surface life will be completely invisible. When taking food of this type, trout must penetrate the surface with their lips.

The tell-tale sign of a surface rise is a ring on the water, often accompanied by a "pop" which is the displacement of a tiny air pocket by water. If the trout are taking a surface insect, the dry-fly box must be consulted and a fly of appropriate size selected. But sometimes the trout are sucking in morsels that are in or just under the surface. These bits of food are sometimes land creatures that drift very close to the surface or in a semisubmerged position. At other times they are submerged mayfly spinners that have completed their reproduction cycle and are drifting along just under the surface film.

For the angler to achieve any sort of results when the trout are taking this form of food, he must really put his best foot forward and do a little preliminary research. The ideal instrument to have along at times like this is a piece of cheesecloth about three feet square. This is used by attaching the cloth to a couple of sticks. Place your makeshift seine in the current, allowing an inch or so of the material to project above the surface. Hold it in the water a minute or so, and then be prepared to make a discovery. If you have never done this sort of "fishing," you will probably be thunderstruck by the number of tiny creatures that have attached themselves to your cheesecloth. Not all of these insects are trout food, but the great majority of them are. By observing the position of the insects on the cheesecloth, it will be possible, to an approximate degree, to determine the depth at which the trout are feeding. The point on the cloth that holds the greatest number of insects will probably be the feeding depth. Check the color and general size of the creatures, and then examine the wet-fly and nymph box. If the trout are taking their food in the surface film or an inch or so under, the same general rules apply as when one is using the dry fly.

The fish will be very critical concerning drag, so an upstream cast is necessary. Again, if possible, use a short line. The strike can be seen or felt more clearly, and your fly can be presented with a gentle cast. If the leader floats of its own accord while your fly remains under the surface, well and good. If not, put a little dressing on it to within a few inches of your fly. (You have already determined the feeding depth.) This floating part of the leader enables you to keep track of the fly's position, and any slight movement of it may indicate a strike.

When casting to a midge-feeding trout drop your fly a good six feet upstream from his location. These tiny flies are nearly always on in great quantities (that's what caused the trout to feed in the first place), and the fish do not have to waste much energy getting them. Try to drift your fly directly over the trout's feeding station. For the reason just mentioned, a trout will seldom move more than six inches to seize one of these small flies. The angler must practically put the fly into the trout's mouth. If he doesn't take it the first time, don't cast immediately back at him. Let your fly drift well past him, and wait a few minutes before trying again. If he doesn't take your offering after ten casts, the chances are very good that he won't touch it at all. Continual flogging of the water is the best possible way *not* to take a midge-feeding trout. If you already have a No. 20 on, this really becomes a problem. Of course, if you have them you may try a 22, or even a 24, but a better alternative would be to trim a No. 18 or 20 until it has a mere suggestion of hackle. Flies of this size are naturally difficult to spot on the water. The angler will find that he is striking at every rise that is within twelve inches of where he thinks his fly should be. This half-blind striking sometimes results in a hooked fish that usually surprises the angler as much as it does the fish.

It should be mentioned here that "striking" with a midge fly is an art in itself. When a trout does gulp in your tiny hook the anticipation quite often causes the fisherman to strike quickly and with considerable force. This ordinarily causes the fly to be pulled from the trout's mouth. The gap on these hooks is very small, and it is quite difficult to make them sink into a trout's hard lip. When the fish takes, it is better to merely take up the slack line and pull gently, rather than make an honest-to-goodness strike. When a trout does take a midge fly he has the utmost confidence in his judgement and usually takes it far back into his mouth. The flesh alongside his tongue is much softer and easier for the tiny barbs to penetrate. In practice this generally holds true, for many midge-caught trout are found to be hooked in this area. Once hooked on an 18 or 20 and handled with reasonable caution, a trout seldom escapes. The midget hooks seem to burrow deeper with each lunge the trout makes. I have examined fish caught on midges where only the eye of the hook was visible, the shank having buried itself completely in the fish's mouth.

To leave the subject for a minute, here's a thought about leaders. The combined experience of many of us has prompted me to believe that it really doesn't matter much to the trout if the leader sinks or floats. This does not, of course, refer to a leader that bounces on the water in tight coils or hopeless snarls. If the leader casts out fairly straight and does not drag, the trout that is about to grab the fly attached to it does not give two cents if it floats or not. I'm convinced that he can see it at all times. In very low or very still water it seems to bother him a bit more. If this is true, the basic reason we turn to finer leaders is that they enter the water more gently and they thread through the eyes of tiny hooks so much easier.

Trout taking these sunken and semisunken tidbits do not seem to waste much energy doing it. They just give their heads a slight twitch to the left or right without moving out of place. Small trout when taking these midge insects will sometimes scurry about trying to catch every one of them. Twelve-inch trout, however, and those of greater size will hang just under the surface and methodically pick their food like the connoisseurs they are. When doing this, they quite often betray their position by making a "hump." At other times there is the familiar ring on the surface that leads the angler to believe that they are surface feeding. In this case, the ring is the result of the trout's dorsal fin or his tail piercing the surface as he turns to resume his station after taking a bit of food.

Try to place your fly or nymph so it floats naturally into his feeding channel. He won't move far to take it, so it must practically be forced upon him. If you can see the fish you are trying for, you will know when he has taken your fly. That slight kick of the head as he turns with the hook is your signal to strike gently. With some fishermen, myself included, this business of watching the fish as he takes a sunken fly has a nerve-shattering effect, especially if the fish is a good one. Only by great self-control can a really gentle strike be made. Ideally, it shouldn't be a strike at all but just an easy pull until the trout's resistance is felt. Naturally it requires practice to do this sort of job nicely, but those of you who have read this far will agree that it is "a labor of love." If the fish in question cannot be seen, the leader must be carefully watched. The slightest movement of it may mean that a fish has taken the fly. In this case, strike with a rapid *pull* but not a jerk—remember those tiny hooks. Quite often trout hooked by one of these really small hooks do not show the slightest bit of concern until you begin to put on considerable pressure. Perhaps he doesn't really feel the bite of that minute barb, or maybe he just can't believe that a "bug" that small could possibly do him harm.

There is a widespread belief among fishermen that the actual pattern used when a small fly is called for is not too important. I cannot go completely along with this line of thought wherever brown trout are concerned. Throughout most of northern Pennsylvania and southern New York, the month of July generally brings a substantial hatch of pale evening duns. The trout take the dun of this insect rather indifferently, but the spinner returning to the water to deposit its eggs is usually taken greedily. These spent spinners lay half in and half out of the surface film as they float helplessly along, supplying an easy meal for the trout. A good fall of pale evening duns can be counted on to put the trout in an extremely selective mood.

For many years I dreaded the nights when the pale evening dun spinners would fall on the waters of the Allegheny River. In spite of the countless numbers of these flies that presented themselves to the trout, the spinners seemed to be a very difficult insect to imitate successfully. The conventional pale evening dun pattern would not even stir a six-inch fish when our "river trout" were picking out this minute mayfly. Many special patterns were tried with small measures of success, but nothing seemed to do the job well. Then one night, Tom Leete, an incurable angling experimenter from Coudersport, Pennsylvania, presented me with a fly that has since proved to be one of the very best late-season patterns I have ever used. It consists of nothing more than an orange-threaded body with a few turns of mourning dove shoulder feather for hackle and a tail of the same material. As with many things of merit, it is an extremely simple creation. Its effect on midsummer trout has been proved to me time after time. It is not a fly to fill your baskets with, for no lure is sure-fire when it comes to tricking low-water brown trout. But it can turn some of those fishless nights into interesting interludes. It is hard to say if this pattern is a dry or wet fly. Due to the softness of the hackle it can be easily used as a wet, and with a little floating dope it can be transformed into a usable dry fly, provided the water is not too rough. I have used this fly in sizes 16, 18, and 20, with most emphasis on the size 18. I am convinced that the orange-threaded body is the secret of this fly's success. The pale evening dun's body (the spinner) actually is a shade of orange, so that *should* be the color that works best. This fly is also a classic on California's Hot Creek.

Very small flies are not generally regarded as being too productive when big trout are concerned. A fishing rule of thumb says that big trout want a big mouthful of fly or lure. This is roughly ninety per cent true. But the time usually comes each trout season when the really small insects make their appearance in such large numbers that even the big trout will be tempted to try them. Of course, fine leaders and tiny hooks are not the best tools for landing a four pounder, but the thrill of hooking him in the first place is nearly as rewarding as is a heavy creel.

BIG WET FLIES

In contrast to the above, if you subscribe to the "big fly, big trout" school of angling, the big fly will take fish without too subtle handling. Big wet flies are most effective fished deep, for they imitate the larger mayfly and stone-fly nymphs that form a staple in the diet of big trout. The pattern selection has never been as much of a problem in deep fishing as that of presenting the fly at the right level in the right places. One advantage of the big fly is that you can see it a great deal of the time and so guide your presentation easier than when using the small sizes. Big flies are effective in off-colored water, for the big fish generally hold down deep in the holes, and all that is necessary is to pass the flies enough times over a given "lie" until the fish decides to take.

Large bulky wets are effective at dusk in the slack shallows of long pools. The trout will often drop down from the fast water under the protective shadows of overhanging trees to search for the big stone-fly and mayfly nymphs. Also they will often mistake a big, slender wet fly for a minnow.

Two or three big flies on a single leader are often effective on rainbows when the fish are lying in broken water at the very tops of pools or the ends of rapids where the water pauses momentarily. Quick motion is not necessary here. Let the current carry the cast across the water. Make several casts over a given location, and work your way downstream a few feet at a time.

Use 2X or 3X leaders, for a heavy strike is necessary to set the hook, especially when striking a big fish.

WESTERN TROUT FLIES

I first learned about western trout and steelhead flies while living back East. A friend of my grandfather's in

Washington state sent the flies to me along with an invitation to fish with him for steelhead at some time in the future.

They were big and almost as gaudy as some of the European Atlantic salmon flies. I tried them out in Esopus Creek, a Catskill river known for its large run of rainbows that harbor all winter in Ashokan Reservoir and ascend the Esopus in the early spring as twenty-inchers.

I fished them as I would the conventional local insect and small-minnow imitations—casting up and across stream and letting them drift and curve directly downstream to then be quickly retrieved. I even dapped them in pairs on the surface along the edges of deep runs. They took rainbows with appealing consistency.

It was not until the war years that I was to fish them in their native waters while stationed at Fort Lewis in Washington. Here I imitated the fishing techniques of friends who wanted me to sample the excellent rainbow, cutthroat, and steelhead fishing that was available only a few hours run from the Fort. After working some of Washington's better streams in winter and summer, I moved after discharge to Portland, Oregon, where I went to work at a radio station. Several of the announcers there were fishermen, and they showed me the Oregon scene from the Deschutes and eastern Oregon streams clear to the Pacific and such rivers as the Trask and the Miami at Tillamook. Here big flies mean big trout. Just what these wet-fly–bucktail-streamer combinations are supposed to represent is a mystery to me. Perhaps they are similar to the big stoneflies and other insects that these migratory fish feed on, or perhaps they look like very young salmon and steelhead.

I always carry a fly box loaded with varied patterns and sizes. They are comparatively simple to tie if you have the ingredients. I have also found that generous ad-libs as to pattern can be in order and that these variations catch just as many trout as the standards. Somehow or other this type of fly is a taker, regardless of pattern, but only if the presentation is normal to the trout. But with all due respect to the western flies, I've found that more exact imitations of the stone-fly, caddis fly, and mayfly nymphs will outdo them most of the time, fished just as they would be on any big stream in the Catskills or Adirondacks or the Pennsylvania rivers. However, the gaudy patterns are excellent in high, fast water that is slightly discolored. In these conditions they should be fished deep and slow.

It is interesting to note that many of the classical eastern trout patterns fare very well on the trout of the Cascades, the Pacific Ocean slope, the High Sierras, and in the waters of the eastern slopes of those magnificent mountains. In the fly shelves in Mark Kerridge's tackle shop in Fullerton, California, one can even find Hardy English-tied flies of ancient lineage along with the stalwarts that were concocted back East in the nineteenth century. So it seems that trout are trout, no matter where they are found. Even the patterns of Ed Sens detailed in the Cycle of the Season, which are imitations of specific mayflies, caddis flies, and stone flies native to most eastern streams, are takers in many of the California streams I've fished. Reports from other anglers fishing these rivers and streams regularly bear out this fact. Presentation of these good old standards seems to be as important out West as it is back East.

I supposed when I moved out to the West Coast that I'd have much to learn, and the techniques I'd learned through years of fishing over the much-pounded trout of the East would be of little avail. So far, such has not been the case. The critical matter of good presentation is the same everywhere. The trout are there; it is our business to present the fly properly to them whether we are fishing New

York's Beaverkill or California's Kings River. To me, only the scenery is different, and it's beautiful on the Kings!

There are, however, a few problems unique to the West. There are specific insect hatches, such as the big stone flies on some of Montana's streams, that require specific patterns if the angler is to enjoy much success. But this is also true on eastern waters. Patterns that are effective in Pennsylvania in May might not take even a chub in Maine's Allagash in July. Brook trout in wilderness streams are a far cry from the "nativized" big browns of the heavily fished streams further south.

One of the most valuable things I've learned fishing from coast to coast is always to lend an ear to the locals—use their patterns when they are available, and when there is time to experiment, try one of my old favorites and see if it produces. The big leverage in marking up high scores is presentation, regardless of pattern, East or West.

On many of the streams of Montana, Idaho, Washington, and Oregon, and to some extent on the streams of northern and middle California, there are some exceptionally large varieties of stone flies, caddis flies, and damsel flies. Some of the caddis flies reach a length of two inches. Add to this the crane flies, dobson flies, and hellgrammites, plus such terrestrials as grasshoppers, and the large western artificials come into their own. The Western Muddler Minnow is a case in point. It is supposed to represent a minnow, but I've taken trout on it while fishing it dead drift on the surface when the large caddis flies were hatching. I've also taken trout with some of the conventional large wet flies, which imitate to some extent the bigger nymphs and underwater forms of these larger insects.

FISHING THE STREAMER FLY

The streamer-fly book houses a veritable spectrum of color—brilliant reds, greens, pastel blues, yellows, silver, and gold. It is very pleasant to contemplate using these gay fellows, for they offer a welcome contrast to the more somber patterns of the nymphs and dry flies.

The manner of fishing the streamer has its special attraction too, for the technique used is unlike that of casting the dainty light No. 12s and 14s. Because of this the stream seems to acquire a new mood; it appears and feels far different when a Mickey Finn or a Parmachene Belle is on the end of the leader. There is the ever-present expectation of a hefty strike.

It is much more than rumor that big trout are taken on streamer flies, and many a whopper that has found itself on an angler's den wall or in the dining room of a sporting camp fell victim to this ruse. Yes, there is a very broad and practical use for the streamer fly in trout angling, and whether it be lake or stream fishing, it is the uninitiated angler who believes that streamer-fly fishing for trout is any less scientific than other forms. When it is realized that almost all trout streams and lakes contain bait fish on which the larger trout feed, the killing qualities of the streamer fly will be recognized.

Big trout obtain most of their food from beneath the surface, and therefore the streamer fly can be fished in a stream or lake at any time when the fish are not actively feeding on a surface insect hatch. Many devotees of wet-fly and nymph fishing know from experience that there are periodic "dead spots" between fly hatches and rely on the streamer during these hours of the day and times of the year rather than resort to a spinner or bait. In the study of insect hatches it is learned that the trout have certain feeding lanes in which they lie and that there are ways of presenting the lure naturally to them. These same rules can be used effectively in streamer fishing.

Streamer-fly fishing first became popular in this country in the state of Maine, where it was proven effective in the lake regions and wilderness streams on landlocked salmon and squaretail trout. These flies were tied to represent the smelt and minnows upon which the trout feed.

The conventional streamer fly is tied in two distinct types, feather streamer and bucktail. The feather streamer consists basically of long hackle feathers tied parallel to the top of the hook shank, extending to or slightly beyond the hook bend.

The bucktail streamer is tied of bucktail hairs or, for that matter, doe hairs or any combination of animal hair which lends itself to attractive action in the water. The material is tied on a long hook shank and extends only slightly beyond the hook bend. Both are called "streamers" because of their streaming, undulating appearance in the water, an attempt to imitate the varied colors and actions of a minnow or small bait fish.

I have lately concluded that exact imitation per se means less in streamer fishing than it does in nymph fishing or dry-fly fishing as far as matching exact colors of the bait fish as we see them out of water is concerned. Certainly no minnow's colors resemble the deadly Parmachene Belle streamer or the killing ancient yellow-and-red bucktail dubbed "Mickey Finn" by John Alden Knight, unless of course the trout are used to feeding on goldfish with high blood pressure! Yet why is it they produce? It would seem that exact coloration is not always necessary. The prime consideration is the action of the lure and its size. The live minnow attracts the trout by its motion, and the man-made minnow should do likewise.

The type of dressing should be selected bearing in mind the general depth of the water and the level at which the lure is to be fished. Sparsely dressed flies on light hooks would be selected for surface fishing in clear water, while in shady spots or early morning and evening fishing, the darker patterns will be seen easier by the trout. Full-bodied flies with heavy hooks would be used when the trout are in deep water or are obviously bottom feeding.

Remember that imitation also plays a significant part in streamer-fly fishing. The black-nosed dace common on eastern streams may not look like a California or Montana minnow. Although the pattern might produce in the West, since any streamer rightly fished will attract the curiosity of a feeding or hungry fish, there are usually patterns devised by local fly tiers that seem to get the job done better. And as I've said often, buy and use the local patterns. Duplicate them at your own tying vise, and if you like, add or subtract a bit from the pattern in order to give a personal touch to the fly if that will give you a little more faith in it. Personal confidence is a big factor in how well a fly will perform. If a fly fits your mood of the moment, use it and fish it hard, long, and well. You'll catch fish with it.

Over the years I've devised some patterns that seem to fit the bill on most of the nation's streams. I illustrate them here along with some notes on their dressing for your guidance in tying. It would be interesting to make a survey in five years or so of anglers who have tried these flies, to see just how well or poorly they have produced. I'm confident I'd get good reports.

All these patterns can be slightly weighted. I prefer to weight them slightly and then, if necessary, to add very small split shot at three points on the leader in order to allow the cast to curve in a wide bow and then turn over. Tied on heavy wet-fly hooks in sizes 8 and 10, these streamers can be fished two or even three on the same leader when experimental angling is in order.

WADING A TROUT STREAM

Duckings can be divided into two classes—those resulting from a lack of wading strategy and those caused by haste or excitement. As an example of the first class, an incident occurred a few seasons back on a fast western stream. The situation involved a pool with a long, shallow reef extending well down the center. Toward the lower end, the reef was surrounded by very deep and fast water. An angler was on the downstream tip and after creeling a nice rainbow, hailed me to look. I had scarcely finished my brief congratulations when he started to head farther downstream. I quickly shouted for him to stop, to return the way he had come. Not heeding the warning, he continued, and a couple of steps later disappeared from view. A few seconds later he was splashing around desperately trying to regain his balance. The fast current actually saved his life, for it quickly swept him downstream into the shallow water where he could gain a foothold and walk ashore. All this time I had been helpless to do anything except catch his drifting paraphernalia—hat, dry-fly box, and rod.

In a similar situation I lost one of the best fish I ever hooked. I had waded to the end of a shelving bar, and my wet flies were drifting well below when the big fish struck. He headed downstream immediately, and when the line was completely stripped from the reel he broke off, leaving me the job of wading back upstream, a tiring proposition, for I had to dodge slippery boulders and fight a roaring current.

Though a ducking can make you very wet, stream wading need not be dangerous if you follow a few simple rules. Aimless wading and a lack of strategy often lead to situations where a return is not easy, where casting is difficult, or where balance might have to be sacrificed to play or land a fish.

One such experience occurred on an eastern stream in a stretch of water running beside a rock ledge. I had gradually moved down along the ledge toward a protruding rock and took up a position in its wash. I soon found that from here I was unable to cast across the stream, so I slowly worked my way out into the deeper water where I'd have more room for a back cast. The current here was very strong, and to maintain my balance while casting required constant concentration.

On one of the upstream casts I hooked into a good-sized rainbow that quickly decided to run farther upstream, necessitating a rapid shifting of my position in order to face the battle. This fellow was active and hard to handle, requiring constant rod pressure and line control. It was during one of his sudden rushes that I unconsciously stepped forward. My footing gave way and I was up to my neck in cold East Branch water, frantically trying to reach a solid footing as the current carried me downstream into the deeper water. I started kicking to find bottom, and in the excitement I forgot the fish but luckily held on to the rod. A hurried glance at the opposite shore revealed that I should head there rather than try to return to the ledge side. I kept searching for the bottom with my feet and when they hit terra firma, I stumbled my way out of the current into the shallows. It was then that I remembered the fish, raised the rod, and gathered in the slack. The trout was still on, though well subdued by this time.

Speaking here as a graduate of the class of fall-ins, I have discovered how important good wading strategy is and how care and caution will make for more pleasurable angling. The first essential of good wading and good fishing is to take it easy and look where you are going. If you are a beginner, it is best to keep to the shallows, advancing to the deeper water with caution. When wading a sandy shore or gravelly stretch, the dangers of falling or tripping are negligible, but keep an eye out for underwater snags and deep holes that might cause trouble. Proceed slowly, placing one foot carefully ahead of the other and keeping the weight on the back or "solid" foot until the "lead" foot is planted securely. If this rule were followed to the letter of the law, falling would be greatly if not almost entirely eliminated. A fall usually occurs because the angler steps or walks from rock to rock and so is unable to maintain a constant balance of weight. When your balance is constant, a slip or sliding motion will, rather than make you feel insecure, actually help you find solid footing.

At the top of a pool the water surface is usually broken and wavy, an indication of underwater rocks and ledges. Stay in the semibroken stretches, for here the water is inclined to be more shallow and so easier to wade. When the current at the head of a pool is fast, stay away from the broken water and select a course where the surface is smooth and not too deep. These spots are usually found in the backwaters or to the side of the main current and can be easily waded while casting ahead and out into the center of the stream. Here again, advance slowly—not stepping, but feeling your way "crablike" and testing the bottom with your feet. If a large rock should be encountered, do not try to walk or clamber over it but skirt the side nearest the shallows. The crotch of even the best of waders is not designed for mountain climbing. Make it a practice never to voluntarily stretch your legs to the limit in order to step or climb over stream obstacles, for it is difficult, if not impossible, to maintain balance in this position, and a slip will throw you overboard.

When wading downstream it is easy to be literally carried away, for the current may be faster and more powerful than you think. Always make it a point to keep an eye peeled toward the shore for an exit route to be used if the going gets too tough. More than once I've been saved an arduous trip upstream by reserving a simple way out of a situation. These exit routes are often good fishing spots, so before proceeding through them, fish the water in advance. Those shallows and bubbly runs sometimes produce a real prize. Make sure, however, that this side water is not too deep, otherwise you will be in the checkerboard position of a double block and the current will throw you every time. If the gravel begins to fall away under foot, start heading for the shallow water where the bottom is more secure.

Suppose, for instance, you are heading downstream and discover that the water is too deep to continue, the current is tugging at your legs, and the bottom gravel has become shifty. It is impossible to go forward or to the left or right—what then? The only answer is to turn around and retrace your steps. Pivot your back foot, slowly turning your body sideways, then point the other foot as far upstream as possible. When half turned around you can gain a full upstream position, breast the current with one hip, and so work your way back. Don't execute this one quickly. Make each move only after your balance and footing are secure.

It is often advisable in downstream work to wade facing sideways to the current, that is, with one foot up-current. I learned this lesson many years ago, but strangely enough, I see very few anglers who use this system. Obviously, bucking the current with one side of your body braced against it is easier than taking it head on. You can master this trick riding in a bus, subway, or train. Try it next time the train starts up or begins to stop. Keep your knees bent, brace yourself by placing the weight on the forward foot, and lean against the pressure.

Whether wading upstream or down, do not head for impossible locations, figuring that with luck you can reach them. You might get there, of course, but is it worth the risk? It is often better to skip over these locations, no matter how fishy they look, rather than chance a ducking. Certainly there are enough good fishing areas on any stream which, if figured out in advance, can be covered safely and easily.

One of my fishing pals is a big, strapping six-footer. He was a star football player not too many years ago and is extremely agile on his feet. He's the kind of angler who makes a game of wading into the toughest spots on the stream. I've seen him reach some of the worst parts of a fast river, and I believe he'd rather tackle these objectives than fish!

Crossing a stream requires maximum care in wading and the utmost in good judgment. First of all, don't even attempt a crossing if there is any doubt as to your ability to cope with the swiftness or depth of the water. Though it may involve a long walk, an easier crossing can always be located. Most of the time a crossing is attempted without an appraisal of the water. Often when the water is shallow at the starting point, the angler neglects to spot a deep run next to the opposite bank until he is almost upon it. He is then in a position where he cannot return upcurrent, so must gamble on those last few feet only to make a frantic grab for a rock or branch on shore just as the current bowls him over.

Select an area where you can cross by wading diagonally upstream, keeping a margin of shallow water below the path of advance. If after starting across, you find you may not make it but the choice of returning or going on is a fifty-fifty proposition, break down your rod with the line still through all the guides, pull your hat on tight, button your jacket pockets and securely tie your wader strings—all you can do now is hope and swear you'll never try it again without first making a keen appraisal of the water.

A wading staff is a great assist for wading in extremely rough water or in stretches where the current is tricky and the bottom is uneven, rugged, and full of holes and awkward channels. The wading staff consists of a staunch pole, not unlike an old broomstick, that in length is about shoulder high. The point should be metal though not necessarily sharp, for it gives added weight and the metal tip will dig into the gravel or lodge firmly between rocks. On the opposite end a strong leather thong is attached through a hole near the top of the staff. This thong is secured to your belt with enough additional length to permit free use of the wading staff. When not in use the staff drifts on the water beside you. The wading staff can be considered a veritable third leg and is often responsible for a safe trip through rough water.

Last season I attempted what seemed to be a tough but possible crossing, and I'll never forget the incident. When I reached the center of the stream I found the current much more swift than I had anticipated, and though I was only knee deep, the upstream wash was splashing my jacket. Slowly I edged my way between the boulders and a few steps farther broke down the rod and battened down the hatches. The next few feet were tough going, and I saw the folly of my decision. I looked back over my shoulder for a possible way of return, and at that instant the stones under foot gave way and I almost went over. That nerve jangler was further intensified when I realized how far I would be carried downstream if I should lose my balance. My wife,

Helen, was on the opposite bank, and the worried expression on her face didn't help matters.

"Don't try it," she yelled, but all I could do was to go forward and hope.

I proceeded an inch at a time and finally managed to reach a large boulder where I placed one foot in the wash. Keeping my knees bent, I brought the back foot forward around the rocks to secure my position. There was only fifteen feet between me and the safety of the bank, but at that moment it looked a mile away! I threw the rod ashore, and sailed my hat into the trees, and got set to do or die. The steady current and constant pressure on my legs and ankles were beginning to have a fatiguing effect, and I knew I would have to make it soon or go for a long, bumpy swim. After trying to advance several times, I found that I was completely stymied. Scanning the bottom, I decided to go slightly downstream with the current in the hope of grabbing on to a rock if I slipped. The gamble worked and gained me a precious yard. My legs were weary, and sharp pains were shooting through my ankles. Helen waded out as far as she could, and believe me, when I managed to clasp her hand, my nerves relaxed for the first time. Once ashore, I found the pain in my ankles becoming really severe, so I stretched out on the bank until they returned to normal. It pays to look where you are going and not gamble on getting there!

One of the difficult elements in wading is the almost constant inability to see the bottom. In the spring this is due to muddy water, but even when the water is clear, sky and foliage reflections interrupt vision. This calls for the ability to read the currents and see with your feet. Here again, it is paramount that you do not step but slide your feet over the bottom to discover any rocks, snags, or sudden drop-offs.

When the water is strange, it is often best to wade in the direction where there is less reflection, and this may mean wading in a different direction than the one you have chosen for your fishing.

A great aid in fishing and in wading, too, is the use of Polaroids, either as nonprescription sunglasses, slip-over lenses for your glasses or Polaroid-ground prescriptions. If you would rather, there are Polaroid shades built into many of the more modern fishing caps. The use of any of these will greatly eliminate reflection glare, making it easier to see into the water.

Quiet pools sometimes harbor large rocks or sudden deep holes that are not exposed by the surface currents or that cannot be seen directly. Move slowly here, placing one foot ahead only after the other has been securely planted. Do not step on the tops of rocks, for they might roll and so throw you off balance. Keep your knees bent, for they act like a spring.

Ernie, one of my most constant angling companions, is not young, and his legs and muscles are inclined to be stiff. He sometimes has trouble staying upright, for he insists on stepping and stomping in the water to obtain a secure footing. Every once in a while the rock turns, and because he is off balance he goes for a swim. He's tried all kinds of foot gear, but I keep telling him that gear will never replace balance. I am continually reminding him to slither his feet along the bottom rather than step, and to keep his knees bent.

From all of this you might think that I always recommend wading the easiest parts of a stream. I do, with this one condition: "subject to angling strategy." Quite often the easiest areas to wade are the places where the fish are lying, and wading through them would obviously put them down. A few minutes spent in observation will reveal the path of approach. If fishermen thought out their advance more thoroughly, they would not ruin good water for themselves or for those who will follow after. I can recall many instances when fish were surface feeding until an angler carelessly waded out among them. Haste in wading makes noise and ripples, especially in pooled-up water, and splashing along in the shallows can do likewise. Two, three, or four anglers that respect each other and move quietly can fish a stretch of water without putting the fish down. My wife and I usually work within forty feet of each other.

When possible, enter a pool from below and start wading in the fast water near the tail, working quietly up the pool well to the side of the stretch to be fished. Approaching in this manner makes it possible to cover the entire pool from all casting angles, yet requires few changes of position. Entering the pool from either side will scare the smaller fish into the deep water, and in their frenzy to reach a safe hiding place they will alert the others and send the lot of them, particularly the biggest ones, into the deep water and under the rocks where they will ignore even the most alluring fly. Trout, especially in overfished waters, watch anything unnatural with an innate distrust and are extremely sensitive to the angler's shadow, reflection, or moving form. Surface disturbance created by careless or fast wading will also put them down. Anglers paying little attention to these facts are the ones who complain about the poor fishing.

Downstream fishing requires a minimum of movement in all but the fastest water because trout constantly head upstream, and their alert eyes are quick to see danger, especially from above. For this reason it is often advisable to work from behind a shield of rocks or against a background of trees. Remember, too, that the deeper the water, the more chance the trout have to see you, for their angle of vision increases with the water depth.

One of the most common angling faults is that of casting the line over the fish, or worse still, having the sunken line drift down through the run that is being fished. This occurs when the angler has failed to scan the water before fishing and chart a course to present the flies without the damaging presence of dragging line. A little forethought will often reveal the strategy of approach and place the angler in a position where a shorter line can be used—always a definite advantage. A careful approach and correct angle of presentation require quiet wading, and it is surprising how close it is possible to get to feeding fish without scaring them.

CHAPTER III
The Sport of Nymph Fishing

NYMPHS AND WET FLIES

Nymph fishing and wet-fly fishing are closely related. While wet flies are basically designed to imitate nymphs, among other things, the reason for the closer "nymph" imitation is that during a specific hatch the trout tend to become finicky, and when feeding on one particular insect species they are most selective. To meet this situation the imitation must go beyond simulation to the faithful reproduction of the nymph in size, shape, coloration, and general over-all appearance. The nymphal imitation is preferred during these times over the more general effect of the wet fly, particularly in clear-water fishing for brown trout in eastern waters. True, wet-fly patterns do produce during these periods too, but I have discovered that when both a wet fly and a nymph imitation of a specific insect are fished at the same time, the nymph usually wins out. The wet fly, on the other hand, is generally a far better producer when a hatch is not in progress or even expected. That is why the wet fly is commonly used as a fish locator, when the angler is casting over all likely places without any plan in mind other than "bumping into" a trout.

The artificial nymph is deadly because it represents the underwater or nymphal stage of our stream-bred insects, the most constant and varied all-season food readily available to the trout.

Nymph fishing is most productive just before and during the hatching periods because the trout feed on nymphs as they are nearing the surface to emerge into the air-borne phase of their existence. The sport rivals any other type of angling, for it is offering the trout the facsimile of what he wants right where he wants it.

You have probably seen trout rising freely yet not taking the dry fly, even though to the casual observer the fish seemed to be surface feeding. I've been confounded by this situation many times, and one afternoon I borrowed a pair of binoculars and watched the water carefully. What those glasses revealed sold me once and for all on the sport of nymph fishing. The fish were taking nymphs just below the surface. All that remained to be done was to tie the proper imitations and learn how to fish them.

The development of nymph imitations started to gain a foothold in this country about forty years ago, when anglers began taking an interest in imitating the living stream insects. Alert fly tiers and later the manufacturers realized the value of these early findings, and at once a number of "nymph imitations" appeared on the tackle counters. Though far from accurate and with little known about their presentation, they were a start in the right direction because they took fish.

It is very unfortunate that much of the angling literature, especially from the earlier British writers, has been taken as gospel over here, for it has created much confusion. English fishing techniques are innocently followed today in America where the fish and the streams are different. With all due respect to those thorough British writers and especially to my friend the late G. E. M. Skues, we must eliminate theories, ideas, and traditions from abroad and learn the basics of our American fishing. A working, practical knowledge based on natural laws will make fishing more entertaining and productive.

As is the case in exact imitation in dry flies, only a small percentage of the thousands of insect species found in or along a stream are of serious consequence to the angler. To be able to recognize these and know their habits is for all practical purposes sufficient. With this knowledge, the angler can take just a few minutes before the first cast or during a lull to examine the specimens from the stream, match the artificial to them, and then confidently proceed to fish.

At first glance one might imagine this to be all-inclusive, leaving no loopholes, and that to proceed this way would result in limit catches every time. I do not wish to convey this impression, however. Nature has a bag of tricks well designed for the protection of her children. There is, however, one constant on which we can depend: the development cycle of a few basic types of stream insects throughout a given season. Though the weather may play tricks, the cycle proceeds close to schedule, and the angler can join in at any point and detect the nymphal species active at the moment, which is a great help towards arriving at the answer to where the fish are and what they are currently feeding on.

Ed Sens, one of the most successful nymph fishermen in the United States, has not only made a practical study of the nymphs and flies of the trout stream and their imitations but over a long period of years has gained valuable experience which has resulted in many a filled creel.

I recall some years ago watching Eddie fishing a streak run below a rapids. The main isle of current was in the center of the stream and gradually slowed down into the pool below, where it was deflected by two large boulders. In a quiet and deliberate manner, he cast a March Brown nymph across to the edge of the main current and, as it drifted down, adjusted the line, paying it out until the nymph was within a few feet of the two large midstream rocks. Very gradually the current drifted the lure in front of the rocks, whereupon Ed lowered the rod tip almost to the water, held it motionless, then, with a slow hand-over-hand retrieve, gradually tightened. The nymph swam naturally and easily to the surface and with it came the sudden flash of a good-sized trout. Ed raised the rod tip ... it was as simple as that!

Following the same procedure he shortly took four additional trout from between the two boulders. Eddie's success here was due to the fact that he knew how and where to fish the nymph—a knowledge gained from observation, study, and streamside application.

In the study of the aquatic insects it is wise to concentrate on the most common species of mayflies, caddis flies, and stone flies and their principal hatches occurring throughout the trout fishing belt in the northern states and Canada. Identifying them, their emergence dates, and general habits will show how important the life cycle of each insect is in relation to your success. Then the how, when, and where to fish the nymph, wet fly, and dry fly will become apparent. When the proper times to imitate the insects are known and recognized, it becomes obvious why nymph fishing and wet-fly fishing can be so very interesting and productive.

MAYFLIES

There has been much more study and consequent imitation of the mayfly nymphs than of either caddis or stone flies. This is most probably because of the existing wet- and dry-fly patterns that have become widely accepted.

The term "mayfly" is a confusing one. Mayflies generally hatch from the beginning of April to the middle of August in the medium trout-fishing belt—New England, New York, Pennsylvania, Michigan, to Washington and Oregon. There are all kinds and sizes of them, so when you hear an angler say the mayflies are hatching, it doesn't mean too much. Most anglers associate the mayfly with the big Green Drakes, one of the largest species. Actually there are some species of a mayfly equivalent to size 20 and smaller hooks.

The mayfly egg develops into a nymph which either clings to a rock, burrows into the mud, crawls or clambers over the stream bottom, or swims in the current. They inhabit certain types of water and definite areas of the stream until the time of transformation into the winged form, or dun (called in scientific terms the *subimago).*

Hatching may occur in the water, on a rock, or along the muddy bank of the stream. After the nymph becomes a dun, it flies away to a tree near the stream to shed its dun skin before returning to the water as an adult or spinner. (This last phase is a peculiarity of the mayflies only.) During this return flight the insects mate, the female's eggs are fertilized, and she deposits them in the water, either by dropping them while gliding over the surface or by actually touching the water with her body. The eggs sink to the bottom and there begin to develop into next season's insects.

It is important for the fisherman to know that the nymph lives a year or more in the underwater, or nymphal, state, but after reaching the dun and spinner stage it exists but a few days, usually one or two, a week at the most. Much has been written for the dry-fly angler about the flying state of these insects, but until recently little fishing or scientific data has been available about this most interesting phase, the nymphal underwater period.

There are four types of mayfly nymphs: burrowers, clamberers, clingers and swimmers. Scientists have grouped them according to their physical characteristics, and each has definite peculiarities as to habitat, hatching activity, and life cycle. All this has its direct bearing on the trout's feeding habits and consequently on the angler's approach.

BURROWERS

The burrowers do just that—burrow in the soft mud and silt of the stream bed. Look for them in the lazy stretches where the current has left silt and ooze in the pockets, snags, and backwaters. Where there is a soggy edge or sloping stream bank, look for small mining marks, similar to mole tunnels, where these insects have gone under. Often the tail and hind parts are partially exposed, and when pulled out and thrown down on the mud they will rapidly burrow again.

The burrowers are the largest of the mayfly nymphs, ranging from one to one and a half inches in length. They are hairy- or fuzzy-looking forms, semi-oval rather than flat, with noticeable mandibles sticking out from under their narrow heads. Their only means of active locomotion is by kicking or flipping upwards as the current carries them along.

From the angler's point of view these nymphs at this initial stage of development are of little importance except when a rain or sudden rise of water washes them into the stream and down into the mouths of hungry trout. They are extremely important, however, when it comes time for them to rise up from the bottom in an effort to reach the surface and hatch.

At hatching time the burrowing nymph rises to cast off its outer shuck in transformation to the winged state, or dun. It is now at its prime from the standpoint of food value to the trout. The nymph becomes very active and must cast off the armorlike suit quickly, for it is now vulnerable to attack from fish and birds. Nature puts it in motion during this period with full steam ahead. Its antics at the surface while casting its shuck and working out its wings and its take-off into the air cause surface disturbance. The trout know all about this story, for they have been following the nymphs or awaiting them in the feeding lanes. Therefore, to be successful the angler must accurately imitate the hatching insect's movements. At this brief stage it is of prime food value and will never feed again but must live on the stored energy.

CLAMBERERS

The clambering mayfly nymph is equipped with legs that carry it about the stream bottom in all kinds of water currents. It depends upon this ability, and constant protection is found amidst sediment and sticks in the trash of the stream bed. The drifting silty substances adhere to its body as an aid to camouflage. The body is a flattened oval in shape and is shorter than that of the burrower. The legs are spindly, equipped with a claw to hold on in the current.

When it comes time for the emergence, the nymph leaves the bottom of the stream and drifts for some distance in a suspended, motionless state, playing possum to avoid detection. It is not too easily recognized while drifting along with bits of dead leaves and sticks, but it is during this drift that it is of particular interest to the trout and the angler.

When the nymph is ready to hatch it must kick its way to the top and, upon reaching the quieter water to the side of the faster runs, cast the shuck.

The dun has some difficulty struggling into the air before flying away to the woods, where it undergoes the typical mayfly stage of development into the spinner to return to the stream in the evening to mate and deposit the eggs.

CLINGERS

The clinging nymphs are found mainly on and around the rocks of the stream, on the underside of rocks, in the sheltered ledges, and on the shady side of sunken refuse. They are equipped with powerful wide legs and strong claws, and in some species there are suction discs on the abdomen to help them hold to the rocks. The body is generally thin, and flat, shorter and more bulky than that of the clamberers. They are largely inaccessible at this stage, except where the trout can root around the rocks and grab at the unwary ones. About the only time they are available before their drift to emergence is when the rocks are rolled or dislodged by sudden spring freshets. This is one reason why nymph fishing and sunken wet-fly fishing is excellent during the early season of high waters.

When the clingers are about to hatch they leave the shelter of the dark rock crevices and undersides to drift in the current close to the bottom. When this "downstream migration" is taking place, the drifting insects avoid the faster currents above. Observation will reveal quiet, still waters and even reverse currents beneath the fast surface, comfortable places where the trout lie in wait for the insects to come downstream to them, and these are the important spots to fish.

At the time of emergence the clingers drift up toward the top in much the same manner as the clamberers. They too are unable to swim in the true sense, but kick their way as they rise. They emerge from the nymphal shuck usually below or right beside a rapids, attracting the attention of any fish in the area, and the bulges and swirls of actively feeding trout will follow.

The duns will appear just to the side of this swift water and drift into the quieter sections to clumsily take off into the air. The spinner transformation then follows with the consequent return flight the following evening.

SWIMMERS (FREE-RANGING TYPE)

The swimmers are the most active of the entire group of mayfly nymphs and can be seen ranging over the bottom to the side of the fast water, leaping and dashing minnowlike in search of food. While wading alongshore in the shallow water I have often mistaken a group of them for small minnows or trout fry. Upon close examination, however, they are readily distinguished. Many wet-fly patterns are designed to imitate this sleek nymph type. They are the most streamlined, smooth-bodied form and are equipped with heavily fringed tails that act as propelling flippers. The gills along sides of the body also help to speed them through the water. Their sensitivity is the most acute of all the mayfly nymphs. They vary in size from one half to one and a quarter inches in length.

CADDIS FLIES

Much of the angling literature bypasses the caddis-fly larva, pupa, and adult. The mayfly has long been glorified by angling writers, and much of the lore of trout fishing, particularly of the dry fly, is centered around the adult insect. There is definite reason for this, as mayflies float for quite a spell before taking to the air and thus give the trout ample opportunity to feed on them. Adult caddis flies, on the

other hand, do not drift on the surface upon hatching but immediately take to the air.

The adult of the caddis fly is of interest to the trout and the angler mainly when drifting downstream as a dead insect and is well represented by many of the downwing wet-fly patterns. The most important stage of the caddis fly, that of the pupal drift and emergence, is of prime interest and can be imitated in pattern and presentation.

Caddis flies are found in most streams and lakes—in many locations that do not contain the various mayfly species. Most of the common species are easy to study while in the worm or larval state, and one need only look into the water to see their little cases of sticks and gravel clinging to the rocks, sunken refuse, and plant stems. Inside these variously shaped cases, the caddis worms are developing. Pick one up and you will see the head and a few feet dangling from the entrance of the case. The insect can either cling to the rocks or crawl snail-like along the bottom, carrying its houselike case with it.

The caddis larva and pupa form a very large percentage of the trout's diet. Throughout the entire season they abound and are readily available when other species of insects may be absent or inactive. In the early part of the season the caddis larva and case is devoured by the trout, and you may have wondered upon cleaning a fish at the amount of gravel and sticks in the gullet. The trout did not take this material into his mouth by mistake; what you find are the remains of caddis cases, the little larval worms inside having been digested.

GREEN CADDIS

One particular insect imitation that is extremely effective in some of our eastern streams, notably those around the

New York City watershed area, is the green caddis, which is described further in the chapter. I have noted for years that trout take these larval worms more than any other underwater type in cold weather, mainly because they are the most available and easiest to get because of their inability to swim or move about. As a worm it can only cling to the rocks or drift at the mercy of the current right into the trout's mouth. Quite naturally, the imitation takes trout when fished drag-free right on the bottom, which to this angler is an important requisite on the first days out when the desire to take fish and keep them is perhaps the strongest of the year. Certainly fish are wanted if we are to brave the cold water and crisp air. It is very surprising that this nymph fished dead drift is much more effective than worm fishing, even when the water is cloudy.

In streams where brown trout are fresh hatchery arrivals, you will find that they will stay in the quieter water, well down from the heads of the pools, or they will gang up in deep holes near the feeding lanes. When the water warms up a bit, they will disperse, having become accustomed to life in the stream, and will move up into the faster water, though still harboring behind obstructions.

On one opening day, Eddie Sens and I went up to Ten Mile Creek and were greeted at our favorite stretch by three anglers who were fishing worms to little avail. In fact they had but two fish between them when we arrived and these only after six cold hours of spinning and worm fishing. Ed was not in the water more than three minutes when he was fast to a nice brown. I worked upstream from him and promptly took a fish on the green artificial. The worm fishermen were taken aback at our success, and when we told them about caddis larvae they became quite interested. I suggested that they open one of their fish and see what the stomach contained. To their surprise they found what we knew was there—green caddis nymphs. I suggested that they rig up with a bare hook, take one of the green larvae and place it on the hook and try their luck.

It wasn't long before one of them had a fish. My next move was to offer them the artificial, which they gratefully took. I am certain that I converted three men to the ranks of nymph fishermen that cold bleak day.

Extensive post-mortem analysis proves what the trout are taking at the moment. On another stream, for instance, they might feed entirely on cased caddis, if those are the most available, even though the green caddis is found in the same type of stream.

The caddis that build cases are fairly easy to recognize. After some months of development in the cased larval state the next stage is that of pupating. At this time the larva seals the case onto a stone or rock with the case opening facing upstream. The insect crawls back into the case and spins a silklike web or screen inclosing the front opening of the case. The larva now becomes semidormant and incases itself in a silken sac or membrane similar to a cocoon. It slowly develops until emergence time when the incased pupa tears away the silken screen and pushes its way out of the outer. case to kick and rise to the surface and drift downstream at the mercy of the stream current. In some situations the membranous sac aids the insect to reach the surface.

This is the time when the angler can reap a harvest with his caddis pupa imitation fished dead drift. The insect tries to rid itself of the sac and during a caddis hatch numbers of them can be seen slithering along the top of the water, heading for the shore or a midstream rock or snag. Others will pop upwards into the air, particularly if they are present in fast, turbulent water, swift boiling stretches, and slick shallow runs. Trout take them on or just under the surface.

In the spring, the wash behind a big midstream boulder is a good place to drift the caddis pupa imitation. Later in the season, when the water is clearer and warmer, midday locations would be in and around the broken riffs and shelving riffles. The edges of the center troughs where the greatest amount of water carries the greatest amount of food should be thoroughly worked.

Look into the water occasionally and you will see them drifting along with bits of refuse. Note the depth at which they are most prevalent and use this as a guide, for the moment, in your fishing.

A sign of the actual caddis emergence is the turning surface rise of the trout. You will see them swirling half out of water as they pick off the emerging pupa. Seldom will you see a real jump, for jumping is never necessary when the trout are feeding on subsurface food.

The adult caddis fly is readily distinguishable from the mayfly in that it has four long mothlike, fuzzy wings, nearly twice the length of the body. When the insect's at rest on the water or on a rock the wings are folded tentlike over the body rather than held erect in the manner of the mayflies. They sport two long, hairy feelers from their heads. Caddis adults have no tails. Their form is not unlike many of our down-wing flies that are purposely designed to represent them, another reason some wet-fly patterns are such famed fish-getters.

Study the emergence time of these flies on your favorite stream or in the general locality you fish, and watch for signs of undersurface feeding activity by the trout.

During the evening the adults from previous hatches may be seen over the stream in droves. (The caddis does not transform like the mayfly to a spinner stage but is a completely developed adult when it emerges from the water.) In this evening flight the female is adorned with the egg sac, generally an olive-green color. Catch one in flight, and very likely the egg clusters will fall off into your hand. One identifying peculiarity of this adult flight is that they invariably head upstream despite the direction of the wind.

The females rarely deposit their eggs in the main stream but crawl into the water, generally down a rock near the shore. At this time wet-fly fishing comes into its own, for many of the insects are swept away in the current before the eggs are laid, and those that do perform die soon afterwards and are carried dead drift near the surface. Wet-fly fishing along the banks and in the quiet backwaters beside windfalls and snags is productive.

The stream may look quiet, but if you are observant you'll see trout gorging themselves near the stream edges, particularly near old windfalls.

STONE FLIES

The stone fly, a clamberer-crawler type, is known in its most prevalent form as the water cricket. There are a great many species of this fly, generally distributed, that hatch at various times of the season. All stone fly nymphs are an ever-constant food supply to the trout, as they are largely bottom crawlers. With the exception of the giant species, they are quick of movement and well designed to hold on to their perch in the fast water as well as scamper off on strong feet to safety. They depend, therefore, on their ability to move quickly when pursued. They are generally found in and around rocks, underslung ledges, and in the trash of backwaters. Their bodies are somewhat flattened and range in size from three-eighths to one and three-quarters inches. They seldom venture far from the darker sections and almost never are found near the top of the water in the company of more active mayfly nymphs. In imitating the angler must learn to fish near the bottom in order to interest the trout.

During the spring washouts some of these insects become temporarily dislodged and are whisked away in the current, yet they are far from helpless, as is the case with many mayfly nymphs. These stone flies can readily return to the safety of the bottom or at least grab hold of a rock.

In sharp contrast to many of the other insects, the emergence of the stone fly is relatively unimportant to the angler, for the majority of the stone flies transform at night and, as their name implies, they hatch on the stones along the stream edge or on large mid-stream rocks. The empty shucks are a common sight on the rocks of all trout streams, so study them for comparison with your imitations.

The fully developed adults then dry their wings in utter safety and fly away to the trees, bushes, and rock crevices nearby. Unless a sudden gust of wind bats these slow, heavy flies to the water, they are totally safe from the trout.

The adult winged stone fly has four equally long, smooth, shiny wings which it folds flat over the back when at rest, not tentlike in the manner of the caddis.

The egg-laying occurs at dusk or after dark, which points up the reason for excellent nighttime fishing, especially during the summer months. There is no necessity for actual nymphal imitations of the many stone fly species, because there is little interest in them at hatching time. At dusk or after dark, large wet flies fished in the shallows or in the tails of the pools can be productive. Throughout the season there are so many of the various species, sizes, and shapes in the stream that it is unnecessary to imitate them exactly.

When the principal species of insects have hatched, there will be occasional scattered insects that will emerge from time to time, but none of these will be of sufficient interest to start a mass feeding period. The wet fly fished on the surface will, however, arouse attention, for it imitates anything of the insect world that has fallen into the water and is drifting or trying to escape. Fishing over the large holes and through the deep aerated runs will be the best technique for success.

The only stone fly that is described in the "Cycle of the Season" section occurs after most of the mayflies have long since hatched and disappeared from the stream.

In the pages that follow I have attempted to put into words the actual situations, conditions, and complete directions for your guidance. Without the made-to-order situations and conditions, vague generalities of technique are useless. If you are able to grasp and visualize the steps and the reasons for them and can "try them for size" on the stream and meet with modest success, I will feel much rewarded. I do guarantee, unqualifiedly, that in following them, especially when they become "second nature," you'll derive more pleasure in your fishing, which is one of the important reasons why this book was written.

With this initial description of the various insect types which make up the trout's food, let us fish through a season from opening day in April through the summer months and weigh the relative merits of nymphs, wet flies, and dry flies, the numberless techniques of their use, and the importance of observation and presentation.

Primarily, the working area is that of the Pennsylvania, New York, and New England streams, but where possible I have lifted specific situations from diary notes of experiences in Michigan, Utah, California, Oregon, and Washington.

CYCLE OF THE SEASON

INTRODUCTION

If the season opens with cold weather and cloudy days, the temperature of the water is bound to hover around 38 or 40 degrees, at least in the areas where the air temperature is between 40 and 50. This situation demands a specific type of nymph angling. When temperatures are this low be prepared for few or no signs of surface feeding. The trout will be found nursing the very bottom of the stream, preferably where they can lie just to the side of the current behind a rock and rest while barely moving a fin. Occasionally, one will point its nose out into the current to pick up 'a passing nymph, but beyond that, they will be loath to move about.

Nymph fishing is good at this time of year, before the first hatch of mayflies, and even though you may see a few tiny stone flies and caddis flies on the surface, keep your nymph on the bottom and let it bump and bounce in and out of the holes and dug-out sections below obstructions and rocks.

QUILL GORDON

Order: *Ephemeroptera*
Family: *Heptageniidae*
Genus and Species: *Epeorus pleuralis*
Nymph Type: Clinger
Nymph Size: Body: ¼ in. to 5/16 in. Tails: two, ¼ in.
Nymph Shape: Flat and broad
Nymph Color: Body: gray-tan. Legs: tan-gray. Wing pads: brownish-black. Tails: medium brown
Habitat: Fast, clear, rocky streams (aerated sections particularly)

NYMPH IMITATION (Sens)

Hook: Size 14 Mustad Viking 94836
Silk: Pearsall's Gossamer Primrose
Tail: Two strands wood-duck flank feather fibers (same length as body)

Body: Gray muskrat dyed light tan (leave untrimmed or pick out with a pin)

Hackle: Light gray-tan, only two turns (clip off top fibers)

Wing Pad: Dark-gray mallard flank feather (clip to shape)

Finish: Whip and varnish

Emergence: Southern New York, Northern Pennsylvania, Oregon, and Washington: April 1 to May 9. Noon or warmest time of day

Dun Size: Body: ⅜ in. Wings: 7/16 in. Tails: two, ½ in.

Dun Color: Body: medium gray with slight yellow cast. Legs: tan-gray. Wings: slate blue-gray (smoky). Tails: medium gray-brown

Standard Dun Patterns: Quill Gordon, Blue Quill, Blue Dun. Size 12 or 14

The little slate-gray mayfly commonly known as the Quill Gordon is the first insect of any importance to hatch and will be in evidence before opening day if the weather has been relatively warm. The sight of these flies on the water is as welcome as the first robin. Though you may doubt it at times as you shiver in your waders, spring is here—the phoebes have arrived, and the song sparrow is in full mating song.

It is a great occasion to approach the stream and tie one of the Quill Gordon nymph imitations on the end of a nine-foot leader tapered to 4X. It will probably be noon before the hatch starts, but prior to this the nymph is a drifter and so will be migrating well down in the water.

Situated on the bank, we are overlooking a fast section of the stream with the main current running in the center. The average depth here is three feet. There are streaks of medium-fast broken water on either side of this current, fanning out toward the edges of the stream. It is in these streaks of medium-fast water that the naturals will be drifting. The trout like this area, too, as it affords good protection and also a vantage point to take the food coming down to them from the main feed flow.

After entering the stream we wade carefully through the slack water to take up a position just to the side of the main current, about a rod's length from the center of it. The plan is to work both the far and near stretches in the same cast.

A short-line cast is called for, upstream and across, well over the main current and slightly beyond the streak of medium-fast water. Immediately when the nymph and leader are on the water, the rod tip is lifted high to keep the line from hitting the central current and thus having the nymph whisked away. As the imitation drifts down into the current the line bellies into the medium-fast water. A strike here will be felt as a slight tug requiring the immediate setting of the hook and will be announced by a sudden movement of the surface line.

After the maximum practical amount of line is used in this situation and is absorbed in the downstream drift, the rod tip is slowly lowered to the surface and is pointed downstream directly at the line. The nymph, due to the action of the current on the line, swings upward from the bottom and crosses into the medium-fast water of the feeding lane. A strike here will require little or no setting of the hook because the line is taut during the rise. This is the most killing time of the whole cast.

The imitation then crosses over the central current swinging in our direction and enters the fringe of the medium-fast water on our side. Again it is in position for a strike, from any trout in this lane. The fly is guided slowly out from the current and drifted into the quieter water as the rod tip is held down. The line is slowly retrieved, hand over hand, until it again is pointing directly downstream, much of it floating on the surface. This action causes the nymph to rise slowly to the top and at this point a strike is felt as a strong tug against a taut line, and to set the hook the rod tip is raised with a sharp snap of the wrist.

If the water is exceedingly fast and heavy, it is sometimes advisable to weight the leader with a very small piece of lead attached about two feet ahead of the imitation.

A bit later we concentrate on another favorite stretch at the head of a large pool just below a rapids. There the main current is again in midstream, fanning out to either bank. However, in this particular case, the pool is too difficult to cover in one cast, so a casting position is found slightly below the point where the main current begins to spread.

Casting again slightly upstream just into the edge of the faster water, we carefully and slowly pay out additional line leaving no slack. The nymph is carried with the surface current away from the fast water and sinks well under as it comes down opposite us. From here it is a simple matter to drift the lure naturally in the outer fringe of the main current. During this drift it can be taken at any moment.

When the line begins to straighten out below, the rod tip is again dropped and pointed directly downstream. The floating line and action of the current cause the nymph to rise gently toward the surface and we see the flash of the trout. Incidentally, if there had been no strike the method of fishing would be to gradually work the nymph back upstream in a hand-over-hand retrieve, letting the nymph rise and fall by guiding it from the fast to quieter water. While angling in this manner I have often had a dashing strike almost under the rod tip.

A short while later, we are at the run where the rapids empty into the big pool. Upon arrival, one, two, three, and then a half dozen of the Quill Gordon duns are drifting on the surface. The hatch is just beginning, which means that the nymphs are drifting close to the top or at least the majority of them are in the upper water preparatory to emerging. There are occasional swirls of feeding trout. Funny thing, you say, but those fish are not taking the floating emerged flies from the surface but are breaking and flashing just the same. Ah, this is an interesting point and one which can confound the dry-fly angler. A close look at the rises shows the trout feeding just under the surface where the nymphs are drifting, completely ignoring the floating duns because at this moment more nymphs are at the surface than emerged duns and are easier for him to obtain.

This calls for a dry-fly type of delivery of the nymph with the addition of a wet Quill Gordon attached to a tippet halfway up the leader, to imitate the insect during the actual emergence. To be more concise, the nymph imitation is used to simulate the drifting nymph while the wet fly imitates the nymph at the surface, casting its shuck during transformation to the dun stage.

Because of the insect's habit of drifting into the quieter water, we now thoroughly work that area too as we move the imitation naturally in the spreading currents.

Up-and-across-stream nymph and wet-fly presentation can be very effective and equals dry-fly angling in the amount of skill needed for successful delivery, and also in results. It is best used to advantage by employing as short a line as possible, holding the rod tip high, while endeavoring to allow the imitations to drift lazily and naturally into the quieter sections. The strike is readily seen, and a flash underwater or a quick turning rise on the surface is followed by the feel of a hit, and another trout is played.

We find upon surveying the pool that many more of the insects are skittering along the top in an effort to take to the air. The peak of the hatch is in progress, and we can see duns disappearing from the surface as the trout begin to feed on them. With their attention now on the duns, the trout have changed their feeding characteristics, and we change to the dry fly.

There is a roll of water and we catch sight of a big fish diving down after having taken a dun from the surface. Motionless, we await a recurrence. Shortly the water bulges again, and the nose and the upper part of the fish's head appear as he glides steadily upward, opens his mouth over the fly, and drops back under again. Our pulse quickens as we carefully deliver the fly a few feet above his position, figuring that a natural surface drift, drag-free, will take it right to him. Everything works well but the expected return of the trout. When the line as well below we retrieve and await another rise to the natural. We do not want to scare this big fellow.

The shadow comes quietly, slowly, and deliberately. The surface water parts, revealing the nose and head coming down on the unlucky dun, and the water closes in again quietly as the fish descends as quickly as before.

Again we carefully cast above him, letting the artificial drift over his nose. Down, down it glides at the mercy of the current, and he comes up to the surface. We see him take a dun not two inches from our fly. What's wrong? Did the leader scare him? Was the imitation lacking?

Shortly he shows again, and our eyes are sharper than ever. The dun is fluttering on the surface, and the trout's rise is a bit quicker this time. In all instances the imitation has been drifting in the orthodox manner of motionless, drag-free delivery. Another rise and he takes a fluttering dun. Evidently he wants action.

Anxiously we try again, realizing that a position well above, out of his sight range, is required in order to deliver the fly correctly.

Facing downstream, we drop the fly about five feet above his position, and when it reaches his domain, the imitation is given a slight twitch. The water opens up as before, and his big mouth closes on the fly. We withhold the setting of the hook until he is well under again, so as not to pull it away from him. On the strike there is a mighty swirl and several minutes later we bend him slightly to fit into the creel.

The above pages of fishing narrative might sound made-to-order, yet I can refer to notes of many seasons when just these things have occurred. In the space of three hours, I've taken fish on the nymph, wet fly, and dry fly—a complete experience and one filled with opening-day joys. It required observation, however, and I recall that before I studied the stream and trout food, I usually ventured forth with no idea of the conditions and had no knowledge which would lead me to the selection of the proper fly type and the manner of using it.

A simple person might conclude from this that I know all the answers. Such, however, is hardly the case. Sometimes we have to work harder than at others and observe with sharper eyes. It is helpful to know *what* to look for, and the fascinating part of it is that it is not necessary to fish blindly. We corral all the fishing lore, experience, and study and put them to work in an effort to give the trout what they want when and where they want it.

But, you might say, there are certainly other species of nymphs and larvae in the stream, especially during the opening days. Why do the fish take the Quill Gordon nymphs? The answer here is that great numbers of this particular insect species are drifting and emerging in the water, freely available to the trout, while none of the others are emerging, so are not as available at this time. The trout, seeing the drifting insects, begin to feed on them, at first well down in the current. As the nymphs work up towards the surface, the trout naturally follow. When the hatch is at its peak the trout feed on the surface and easily turn to the emerged insects that drift over their heads.

Quite possibly trout could have been taken on wet flies of almost any pattern. We could have used worms with results or streamers could have produced. It is always possible, and sometimes necessary, to fall back on the trial-and-error method of throwing everything in the book everywhere on the stream, but somehow it is more exciting to be able to analyze the activity on the stream and so design our attack.

The Quill Gordon can be counted on to offer the first real nymph, wet-fly, and dry-fly angling activity of the year. This is true in the northeastern states and the faster Pennsylvania and New Jersey streams, especially those that are rocky and spring-fed. You'll also find similar flies in the upper reaches of the Logan River in Utah and in the countless streams of Oregon and Washington. The middlewestern states of Michigan and Wisconsin also have excellent hatches of similar insects. In all cases the hatch is of brief duration unless a succession of cold days strings it out longer.

HENDRICKSON

Order: *Ephemeroptera*
Family: *Ephemerellidae*
Genus: *Ephemerella*
Species: *subvaria, invaria,* and *rotunda* (similar and appearing together)
Nymph Type: Clambering
Nymph Size: Body: ⅜ in. Tails: three, ⅜ in.
Nymph Shape: Semiround
Nymph Color: Body: ruddy tan. Legs: tan, dark mottled. Wing pads: gray-tan. Tails: mottled tan
Habitat: Slower sections of fast streams and most semiquiet areas

NYMPH IMITATION (Sens)

Hook: Size 14 Allcock 04991
Silk: Pearsall's Rust-colored
Tail: Three wood-duck flank feather fibers
Body: Gray muskrat fur, dyed light tan (untrimmed)
Hackle: Light gray, dyed light tan, just two turns (clip off top fibers)
Wing Pads: Black-duck or moor-hen brown-black covert feather
Finish: Whip and varnish
Note: See Dark Hendrickson nymph pattern
Emergence: Southern New York, Michigan: April 20 to May 15. Early afternoon
Dun Size: Body: 5/16 in. to ⅜ in. Wings: ½ in. Tails: three, ⅜ in. to 7/16 in.
Dun Color: Body: medium ruddy brown. Legs: gray-tan. Wings: medium iron-gray. Tails: tan-gray
Standard Dun Patterns: Hendrickson (Light), Whirling Dun. Size 12 or 14

HENDRICKSON

Right on the heels of the Quill Gordon and sometimes during the Quill Gordon hatch, if the weather is balmy, you will see the next important of the mayflies, which are well represented by the Hendrickson pattern. Seasonally speaking, the Hendricksons lets the Quill Gordons "break the ice" and then follow along.

The Hendrickson hatch occurs during a period of changeable weather, ranging from cold blustery days to tastes of summer. If you fish a local stream each year, it is interesting to take notes on emergence dates.

In aerated streams that are spring-fed and cold, and in the case of some Catskill streams such as the Neversink, the Hendrickson often does not appear in the upper reaches until the first part of May. Out in Utah, the lower part of the Logan River produces hatches of similar insects three weeks to a month before they appear in the higher streams and mountain tributaries. Another similar insect, though a trifle larger and with an olive cast, is found in the Deschutes River in Oregon, hatching in the colder sections as late as June 15. One year while I was fishing on the Rio Grande between Santa Fe and Taos, a sudden warm streak produced Hendrickson-like hatches through the last two weeks in March and the first week of April.

The dun of this mayfly, a trifle larger than the Quill Gordon, is also drab from a distance but very pretty when viewed at close range. The wings are held erect and are of a medium iron-gray color, and the body is a medium tan with tan-gray legs. Both the male and female are readily distinguishable from the slightly smaller and predominantly iron-gray color of the Quill Gordon.

The name "Hendrickson" was given this fly imitation by a famous fly tier in Liberty, New York—Roy Steenrod, State Conservation Inspector. It was named after the well-known angler Albert Everett Hendrickson of Scarsdale, New York, for whom Theodore Gordon also tied flies. Primarily an eastern pattern, it should be a coast-to-coast standby in the northern trout belt. Several similar patterns have become famous because they have been tied by well-known fly tiers in various sections of the country. None of these patterns in the dry fly accurately resembles the insect, but they have been found killers in their various localities during this hatch. There should, however, be little variance in the color of the nymph imitation.

Look for the Hendrickson nymph and fish the imitation in the same type of water as the Quill Gordon. The Hendrickson's natural habitat is the semiquiet gravelly shallows of slower water in the open stream. The nymph is of the clambering variety and is predominantly dark brown-black with brownish-black wing pads and dark black-brown legs. This nymph does not require water that's as pure or as oxygenated as the Quill Gordon does, and I would like to point out here that while the Hendrickson is second in the mayfly cycle, it is the first to appear on warmer streams that may be unfitted for the Quill Gordon. For instance, a lowland stream flowing through flat open country warms up very quickly in the springtime, therefore the Hendrickson is often the first mayfly to appear on this type of water. (Sometimes the Quill Gordon is found in the stream before the season opens.)

The Hendrickson hatch is easily spotted in its locale. Hendricksons hatch in droves. There is nothing timid or sporadic about the hatch. When it starts, it starts all at once, and the air above the stream is filled with duns.

In the evening when the Hendrickson spinners are ready to lay their eggs, the female will be recognized by the prominent yellow egg sac at the base of her tail. Unlike many mayfly spinners, Hendrickson spinners do not touch the water, for they drop their eggs while gliding close over the surface. When the trout are jumping for them it is time to use the Hendrickson dry fly, and if you prefer an exact imitation of the female spinner, try the Hendrickson egg-sac pattern either wet or dry, tied sparse.

I recall an opening day on one of the lower New York State streams when a Hendrickson hatch produced a limit catch and many released fish. I relate this experience here because it is so typical of the Hendrickson as applied to warmer and slower streams.

The opening hours of the day were blustery and cold with the thermometer hovering around 40 degrees. Casting was difficult because of the wind and wading a cold proposition.

When we entered the stream there was no sign of trout activity and no flies on the water. The bloodroot was in full bloom along the verdant green banks, and the trees were just budding into colors of rose and light yellow. The magnolia blossoms were about half out, reminding me of what Ed Sens had said during a winter evening of fly tying: "Look for the Hendrickson hatch on the lower streams when the magnolias are about to hit full stride."

I tied a Hendrickson nymph on a weighted nine-foot leader, figuring that I could use it unweighted when and if I spotted any nymphs drifting in the current. I took up a position at the head of a long broken run where the water sped rapidly between the large boulders and rock ledges. Surveying the area below, I selected a channel of current to the side of the broken water and cast a nymph at the head of this run, keeping slack line for the drift in the left hand. The weighted leader and the speed of the current bounced the nymph gently along close to the bottom.

I fished a taut line in order to feel any strike yet still be able to guide the nymph along the run without exerting unnecessary manipulation foreign to this type of drifting hatch. From this position I was able to work the run and move the lure into the quiet water and into the various pockets and runs where the trout should be lying. While concentrating on one particularly fishy-looking spot, I felt a hit and was fast to a nice brown. Typical of his species, he did not run or dash but stayed right in the deep pocket behind a jagged boulder. I could see him thrashing back and forth in a vain effort to shake the hook, but when I tightened on him

An Assortment of Typical Wet Flies

Standard Wet Flies

1. Brown Sedge
2. Claret Gnat (chenille)
3. Pale Evening Dun
4. Teal and Black
5. Grizzly King
6. Claret Gnat (silk)
7. Red Quill Spinner
8. Brown Woolly Worm
9. Seth Green
10. Snipe and Yellow
11. Greenwell's Glory
12. Wickham's Fancy
13. Black Spider
14. Tom Leete Fly
15. Iron Blue Dun
16. Orange Fish Hawk
17. Alder
18. Brown Hackle Peacock
19. Gray Woolly Worm
20. March Brown
21. Leadwing Coachman
22. Mallard Quill
23. Gold Ribbed Hare's Ear
24. Gray Hackle Yellow
25. Light Cahill
26. Black Gnat
27. Dark Cahill
28. Lady Beaverkill
29. White Miller
30. Pink Lady

An Assortment of Typical Wet Flies

Steelhead Flies

1. Umpqua Special
2. Black Prince
3. Golden Demon
4. Burlap
5. Skykomish Sunrise
6. Thor
7. Skunk

Western Flies

1. Mormon Girl
2. Rio Grand King
3. Carey Special
4. Fledermaus
5. Western Bee
6. Picket Pin

Steamers and Bucktails

1. Red Trude
2. Nine Three
3. White Marabou
4. Muddler Minnow
5. Little Rainbow Trout
6. Micky Finn

Sens Nymphs

1. Gray Fox
2. Brown Drake
3. Giant Stone Fly
4. Little Marryat
5. Light Cahill
6. Green Caddis Pupa
7. Quill Gordon
8. Grannom Caddis Pupa
9. March Brown
10. Green Drake

Standard Wet Flies

Steelhead Flies

Western Flies

Steamers and Bucktails

Sens Nymphs

he quit these tactics and started for the safety of his lair. I raised the rod tip and brought him to the surface—a fine, plump fifteen-incher. Anxious to discover the menu of the morning, I cut him open, finding that he had been feeding on Hendrickson nymphs exclusively. I was not fishing a theory then—the evidence was in hand.

At eleven o'clock the sun was a bit warmer, and though there were nymphs drifting in the current and a few duns on the water the fishing was absolutely no good. Try as I would, I could not get a rise. The only conclusion I could draw from the situation was that the fish had previously gorged themselves to the limit and were taking time to digest their food of the morning.

At two o'clock things were different. Trout activity had started again, and I had just spotted an increasing number of duns on the surface when, as if by a signal, hundreds of tan-gray duns appeared floating down the pools and runs like tiny sailboats in the sun. The rise was on; it was time to switch to the dry fly. I put on a Hendrickson pattern of my own creation and took several large trout. The peak of the hatch came at 3:45. Eddie had said to look for it at 3:30 if the weather was cold with intermittent sun. That was timetabling it pretty well.

I again opened a fish, and an examination of the stomach contents revealed the pattern events of the day. Toward the top of the gullet were the duns. Further down in the stomach were partially digested Hendrickson nymphs, and at the very bottom a few caddis cases of sticks and stones, indicating that the trout had fed exclusively on the bottom during the early morning hours.

The following day, Ed Sens and I fished another stream with equally interesting results. Starting off, we employed the nymph and weighted leader until about ten o'clock, then worked an unweighted one, and finally ended up by using the dry fly. The more I fish, the more I realize that a full creel is not dependent upon luck but involves the simple basic strategy of giving the trout what they want where they will take it.

DARK HENDRICKSON

Order: *Ephemeroptera*
Family: *Leptophlebiidae*
Genus: *Leptophlebia*
Species: *cupida*
Nymph Type: Clamberer
Nymph Size: Body: 7/16 in. Tails: three, 7/16 in.
Nymph Shape: Semiround
Nymph Color: Body: dark blackish brown. Legs: blackish brown. Wing pads: black-brown. Tails: black-brown
Habitat: Quiet water, back eddies near the fast water

NYMPH IMITATION (Sens)

Hook: Size 12, 3X long Allcock 04991
Silk: Pearsall's Rust
Tail: Three ends of moosemane (two black, one brown). Use the rest for body.
Body: Build up body with three layers of Pearsalls Stout Floss (tan or brown) and wrap moosemane forward over this.
Hackle: Dark rusty dun, two turns (clip off top fibers)
Wing Pads: English moor hen or black duck, brown-black upper-wing covert feather (clip to shape)
Finish: Whip and varnish
Note: In most streams this pattern works well for Light Hendrickson.

Emergence: April 25 to May 9. Afternoon. Southern New York, Pennsylvania, Michigan
Dun Size: Body: ½ in. Wings: ⅜ in. Tails: two, ½ in.
Dun Color: Body: dark black-brown. Legs: black-brown. Wings: dark iron gray. Tails: dark brown banded
Standard Dun Patterns: Dark Hendrickson, Whirling Dun, Black Quill. Size 12

DARK HENDRICKSON

This nymph is one of the more common of the mayflies and lives in much the same type of water that harbors the Hendrickson.

Fish the Dark Hendrickson nymph in the shallows beside the fast riffles in and around the back eddies. It is primarily very slow cross-and-down-stream drift fishing.

The duns emerge to the side of the fast water in more or less the same locations the Hendrickson duns select. They are often seen hatching at the same time as the Hendricksons. In the streams where the Hendricksons are not found, they take their place.

I recall a red-letter day on the Norwalk River in Connecticut when I fished a stretch of water about fifty yards below the Iron Bridge, near the little town of Wilton. After tying on one of my best black-brown wet flies I began to cast dry-fly fashion upstream and slightly across the current toward a deep run along the opposite bank. After covering the water thoroughly, I was rewarded with a couple of small hits but failed to connect. I enjoyed the twittering of the birds and the sight of the brave green leaves poking their tiny heads into the spring sunshine. As is often the case, my mind drifted off to these streamside distractions, so I was hardly prepared for the rude awakening as another trout hit the fly and securely hooked himself. Upon later examination I found him crammed to the very gullet with small black-brown nymphs similar to the fly on which I had taken him.

Last year I fished that same water again in April and identified the insect as *Leptophlebia cupida* and enjoyed some nice fishing with the Dark Hendrickson nymph and dry fly.

This insect species is prevalent on the Big Beaverkill, and many anglers sometimes call this the "shad fly hatch" when it appears in late April or, in a cold season, in the first week of May.

I have found the Dark Hendrickson nymph to be more effective than the Light on the streams I fish. To discover the most killing pattern for the streams in your locale, I suggest that you fish both at the same time, first attaching the Light Hendrickson nymph to a six-inch tippet halfway up the leader and then reversing the order, as the nymph on the end always has the advantage.

DARK CADDIS

Order: *Trichoptera*
Family: *Leptoceridae*
Genus: *Psilotreta*
Species: *frontalis*
Case Type (Larval Stage): Pebbly, sometimes with a mixture of sand and refuse
Pupal Hatching Stage Size: Over-all length ⅜ in. to ½ in. including sac
Color: Head, wing stubs, and upper body: dark brownish black. Lower (pupal sac): dark-brown body color surrounded by gray translucent sac
Habitat: Slower-moving water

PUPAL IMITATION (Sens)

Hook: Size 14 Mustad Viking 94840
Silk: Black
Tail: None
(Note: The tying of this pattern is so different from the mayfly nymph patterns that it requires more detailed explanation.)
Body and Sac: Start with a body of stout silk floss. For the grayish pupal sac, spin over the underbody a silver-gray muskrat fur which is picked out to represent translucency.
Head, Hackle and Wings: Two turns of condor quill tied in by butt ends just ahead of pupal sac, but leave remaining quill free and pointing toward the eye of the hook. For the wing, select a small black-duck wing covert feather. Cut tip of feather in shape of a V with the lower stem left on for tying in. Place so that the wings fall to the sides of the body nearly to the end of the sac. Hackle with one turn only of rusty dun. Clip off the top hackle fibers. Wind condor quill to eye of hook, making the head. Whip and varnish.
Emergence: May 1 to 30. Across the country, any time of day—afternoon and twilight especially.
Adult Size: ⅜ in. over-all length
Adult Color: Brownish-tan wings and dark brownish-black body
Standard Patterns: Alder or dark-brown downwing wet flies. Sizes 12 and 14.

DARK CADDIS

When great numbers of the dark caddis are present on the water and several rising fish are seen, it would seem that a dry fly would be the order of the day. However, if results are not forthcoming, watch closely the rising action of the fish, for usually trout prefer to take the caddis pupa on its drift surfaceward rather than the emerged and flying insect. It is easy to mistake the "follow through" for a rise to a surface fly. For many years I was at a decided disadvantage in such a situation, and it was only after working one of these surface hatches with Eddie that the problem was solved.

Many years ago Ed tackled the situation and went to work via entomological books to learn the caddis life cycle. From here he made a succession of trips to the stream for careful examination of the living insects and proceeded to tie the caddis pupa imitation and further study the importance of presentation.

The larvae of this caddis can be easily seen dragging their cases over the bottom of the stream. Later, when drifting in the pupal state, they are rather difficult to spot. It is only at this drifting period that the pupal imitation will produce, because while the trout can take the available drifting pupa they cannot reach the adult insects for, on emergence, they take off immediately. Make sure that the caddis flies seen are actually hatching, because sometimes the adults, although flying about, are those that hatched the night before and so, naturally, none of the drifting pupa will be in the water. Remember that the dark caddis hatches in droves and there should never be any mistake as to whether there is an actual hatch in progress.

When a few of the dark caddis adults are seen emerging it is the tip-off that the hatch is starting. Considerable underwater trout activity will be noticed, and it is now time to dead drift the pupal imitation through the area. After thoroughly greasing part of the leader, cast upstream and across into the semiquiet feeding lanes, drifting the imitation in and around rocks.

The emerged insects are slow fliers, and will be seen in clusters throughout the day, fluttering along the stream bank, many in the act of laying their eggs. They seem to like to be near the water, and do not fly away into the woods in the manner of the mayflies. I have often noted them hovering along undercut banks and around exposed tree roots and rocks. Many of them are caught in spider webs that are suspended over the stream. Wet-fly fishing along the stream edges, especially if there are trouty-looking holes nearby, is bound to produce at this season.

Toward evening the males and females fly out over the center of the stream runs, always heading upstream. The females are marked by a prominent olive-colored egg sac. Try the conventional brown-colored wet fly in size 12 and fish it dead drift along the stream edges where the insects are laying their eggs under the water.

Last year during one of these hatches on the Ten Mile, a stream less than a hundred miles from New York City, I had some of the most productive fishing I have ever experienced.

The insects had just begun to show a few at a time, and in a particularly long fast run I could see the trout rolling a foot under the surface, occasionally breaking water. Casting the pupal imitation well above the activity, I let it drift through the area on a rather slack line. I took a trout on almost every drift, and their gullets contained caddis pupae, some of them with the fragile pupal sac still intact. Chubs and largemouthed bass were also on the feed and took the imitations readily.

GRANNOM CADDIS

Order: *Trichoptera*
Family: *Rhyacophilidae*
Genus: *Rhyacophila*
Species: *lobifera*
Case Type (Larval Stage): Wormlike

Pupal Hatching Stage Size: Over-all length ½ in. including sac

Color: Greenish tinge to body in sac; upper body dark brown

Habitat: Slower-moving sandy stretches of the streams

PUPAL IMITATION (Sens)

Hook: Size 14 Mustad Viking 94840

Silk: Black

Tail: None

(Note: The tying of this fly is so different from the mayfly nymphs that it requires more detailed information.)

Body and Sac: Start with the body of floss and for the greenish pupal sac, spin over the underbody an apple-green wool (very fine) which is picked to represent translucency.

Head, Hackle and Wings: Two turns of condor quill just ahead of the pupal sac, leaving ends free and pointing towards the hook eye. Wing with a small black-duck wing covert feather (cut tip of feather in the shape of a V). Place so that the wings fall to the sides of the body nearly to the end of the sac. Hackle with one turn of rusty dun tied over free condor quill fibers (clip off top hackle fibers). Wind remaining condor quill to eye of hook to make the head. Whip and varnish.

Emergence: May 1 to 30. Across the country, any time of day. Especially late afternoon and until dark

Adult Size: ⅜ in. to ½ in. over-all

Adult Color: Brownish-tan wings and greenish-tan body, dark-brown head

Standard Patterns: Brownish-winged wet flies with variations of tan-olive bodies

GRANNOM CADDIS

The larva of this caddis does not have a case but creeps about naked on the underside of stones and in the sheltered riffles until it reaches the pupal state. As such they are known as "rock worms," and you may see the trout flashing and turning sideways to nose them from the stream bed. When the larva reaches a permanent spot in some crevice, it walls itself in by building a pebble fort. It then spins a tan- or parchment-colored cocoon and there develops until hatching time. When the pupa rises to the surface in its cellophanelike sac, it is of a pale green color. The angling technique, as with all caddis pupa imitations, is dead drift in the main feed-lane currents and in and around obstructions where the trout are lying in wait. Note that the emergence dates for this fly cover a long period, but on certain streams this hatch of Grannoms is usually around the same time each year.

MARCH BROWN—AMERICAN

Order: *Ephemeroptera*
Family: *Heptageniidae*
Genus: *Stenonema*
Species: *vicarium*
Nymph Type: Clinger
Nymph Size: Body: ½ in. Tails: three, ⅜ in.
Nymph Shape: Moderately flat
Nymph Color: Body: cream tan banded with rust brown. Legs: cream tan banded with brown. Wing pads: dark brown. Tails: rust brown
Habitat: Moderate to fast water amid rocks

NYMPH IMITATION (Sens)

Hook: Size 12 Mustad Viking 94840

Silk: Pearsall's light rust

Tail: Three red-brown fibers (cinnamon turkey tail) or three rusty fibers from shoulder-feather fibers of cock pheasant

Body: Sandy-colored rabbit fur picked out with needle (include guard hairs). Ribbing: gold tinsel

Hackle: Partridge, two turns (clip off top fibers)

Wing Pads: Section of medium gray-brown hen pheasant wing covert with prominent tan stem (clip to shape)

Finish: Whip and varnish

Emergence: Central New York, Northern Pennsylvania, Montana, Oregon: May 15 to June 15. Midday and sporadic according to weather

Dun Size: Body 9/16 in. Wings: ⅝ in. Tails: two, ½ in.

Dun Color: Body: alternate bands of cream and rust brown. Legs: cream banded with rust brown. Wings: light gray mottled with black and an over-all light tan-olive cast. Tails: rust brown

Standard Dun Patterns: March Brown, Bradley Special. Size 12

MARCH BROWN

Through the winter the March Brown nymph, in company with the Quill Gordon, has been clinging to the undersides of rocks and gravel found in the faster water of the stream. Through the dark, bleak weather, when to all intents and purposes our stream has been asleep, he has been living his precarious underwater life. Spring freshets threaten to dislodge him. Other nymphs such as the carnivorous stone flies lie in wait for him. Hungry trout are ever-present and ready to take him when he is off guard. During his growing period he sheds eleven shucks.

In the month of May the stream receives more light from the higher sun, and there are warm spells in the current. The wing cases on the nymph's shoulders have begun to develop and turn from a rust color to a deep dark-brown, the preparation for the wings-to-be in future adult life. Comes the time of emergence, the nymph releases himself from his rocky home along with countless others of his clan and begins to drift helplessly in the bottom currents and side waters of the stream, working his way ever nearer to the surface. He kicks and squirms in his armor in an effort to shed the shuck. When partially freed he sometimes skitters on the surface, while attempting to keep his equilibrium, then with a final burst of power, he casts his shuck and transforms to the March Brown dun. He flutters dangerously on the surface of the water and after two or three attempts finally rises into the air and heads for the safety of the bushes and trees that border the stream. There he rests for a few hours, now a beautiful dun.

During the emergence he may have floated fifty or a hundred yards downstream before finally flying away.

The March Brown is one of the easiest of all the species to identify. It is the largest of the flies in the cycle of the season thus far and is easily recognized as a mayfly. Note that the wings, usually upright on most mayflies, are slanted back about halfway down over the body. The insects are generally of a cream and rust-brown color with grayish mottled wings and speckled legs.

The March Brown dun has one more stage of development, that of shedding the dun skin to become a spinner before the search for a mate. This is accomplished in the comparative safety of the woods, but he must hurry, for as a flying insect he cannot feed again. The energy stored in him while a nymph must carry him through to the end.

Finally the dun costume is shed. He is the same shape as before, but his wings, instead of being cloudy, have a glossy transparent sheen, as does his semitransparent body. He is now able to fly about much more rapidly and zooms into the twilight in search of a mate. Twilight finds hundreds of his kind in the air, as they have awaited the cool of the evening for the nuptial flight.

He selects a mate, and they fly together above the stream for some distance until the female's eggs are fertilized, and thus his purpose in life is at an end. The female leaves him, and in the next few minutes the eggs develop to maturity. She seeks a riffle, usually near the head of a pool, and repeatedly touches her body to the water, depositing the eggs. Both of the insects then dance and zoom over the stream until they die and fall into the water as spentwings. Some of the eggs attach themselves to the gravelly stream bed, and some fall between the rock crevices where they attach themselves to develop into the next nymphal cycle.

If we bear in mind this life story, the fishing technique becomes readily apparent and is similar to that used in fishing the Quill Gordon nymph but with far different general conditions. We do not have the heavy, fast, and discolored water of opening day, so much more care should be exercised in every step of the fishing. Avoid unnecessary casting, be careful in the presentation, and use light, long leaders.

This is the season when most of the wild flowers are in full bloom, and the air and bushes near the stream are alive with all species of sparrows, warblers, finches, vireos, phoebes, and wrens. It is apt to be a changeable time of the year, the weather neither spring nor summer but a combination of both. On many a May afternoon I have found myself running for cover just in time to avoid a cloudburst accompanied by sudden winds that whip themselves up to a veritable gale. Yet another day will produce extreme heat that threatens to parboil you alive in your waders!

Any angler and true lover of the out-of-doors cannot help but enjoy watching the emergence of the March Brown and other insects, especially when acquainted with the basic story of their life. It is also comforting to know that the countless species of flies are going to be developing the entire season. Every day the drama goes on. Each week of the season there is another cast of characters, and in some cases there is an overlap of species which causes a grand show of aerial fireworks and acrobatics.

GRAY FOX

Order: *Ephemeroptera*
Family: *Heptageniidae*
Genus: *Stenonema*
Species: *fuscum*
Nymph Type: Clinger
Nymph Shape: Moderately flat with shoulder
Nymph Color: Body: cream banded with amber. Legs: same. Wing pads: dark brown. Tails: amber brown
Habitat: Fast water amid rocks and gravel

NYMPH IMITATION (Sens)

Same as March Brown Sens imitation though a trifle lighter in color. (See March Brown.)
Hook: Size 12 Mustad Viking 94840
Silk: Tan
Tail: Light rust-brown fibers
Body: Lightest sandy-brown rabbit fur

Hackle: Light partridge, two turns (clip off top fibers)
Wing Pads: Gray-brown mallard flank feather (clipped to shape)
Finish: Whip and varnish
Emergence: June 1 to June 15 (sometimes earlier with March Brown). Central New York, Northern Pennsylvania, Montana, Oregon. Late afternoon
Dun Size: Body: 9/16 in. Wings: ⅝ in. Tails: two, ½ in.
Dun Color: Body: alternate bands of cream and light amber. Wings: light gray with dark-gray mottling and light pale-olive cast. Legs: cream banded with light amber
Standard Dun Patterns: Gray Fox, Light Ginger Quill, Light Bradley Special. Size 12

GRAY FOX

Sometimes overlapping the March Brown, the Gray Fox is every bit as important to the angler. This is the period just prior to the entrance of the summer mayflies to the scene, for the Quill Gordons have long since been forgotten and the Hendricksons are through.

The nymph habits and life cycle of the Gray Fox are very similar to those of the March Brown. The Gray Fox nymph is somewhat smaller. Fish a size 12 and you will be on safe ground. The nymph imitation and therefore the wet-fly imitation are so similar to the March Brown that either pattern will suffice.

Insect color intensities vary somewhat in these two species. For instance, a light phase of the March Brown dun is difficult to distinguish from a dark phase of the Gray Fox, so here again some experimentation is in order. Fish both nymphs on the leader and reverse their positions from time to time. For further experimentaion during the hatch, switch the upper nymph to a wet March Brown and work this upper fly on or near the surface where you see the naturals emerging. Work the cast in the edges of the fast water, letting it pause occasionally to drift down to a fresh area.

As far as dry-fly patterns for the floating duns are concerned, I have seldom had experience which would definitely point favorably to one pattern over another. Generally, if the day is dark and overcast, the March Brown seems to do better and on bright days, in exceptionally clear water, the Gray Fox has accounted for some exceptional fishing.

GREEN DRAKE

Order: *Ephemeroptera*
Family: *Ephemeridae*
Genus: *Ephemera*
Species: *guttulata*
Nymph Type: Burrower
Nymph Size: Body: ¾ in. Tails: three, ⅜ in.
Nymph Shape: Semi-oval, fuzzy
Nymph Color: Head and thorax: cream. Abdomen: cream-white. Legs: white to cream (sometimes yellowish). Wing pads: medium brown. Tails: cream
Habitat: Quiet water of streams, lakes, and ponds

NYMPH IMITATION (Sens)

Hook: Size 12, 3X long
Silk: Cream
Tail: Cream, pale webby saddle hackle tips trimmed short
Body: Pale-cream fox fur (fluffed out generously)
Hackle: Cream webby hackle, two turns (clip off top fibers)

Wing Pads: Very small, light, marginal wing feather of hen pheasant (clip to shape)

Finish: Whip and varnish

Emergence: May 25 to June 15. (In some Northern areas these flies hatch well into July.) Pennsylvania, New York, New Jersey, Michigan. From noon on

Dun Size: Body: ¾ in. Wings: ¾ in. Tails: three, 1 in.

Dun Color: Body: head and thorax mottling of brown, black, and cream. Abdomen: cream banded with brown. Legs: creamish tan. Wings: faint greenish tinge on gray-tan mottling

Standard Dun Patterns: Green Drake, Rat Faced McDougal. Sizes 8 to 10

Standard Spinner Patterns: Coffin Fly, White Wulff

GREEN DRAKE

The Green Drake is one of the largest of the mayflies to appear on the trout-fisherman's stream, seldom, if ever, emerging in any number before June in the central trout belt and later in the northern streams. Exceptionally hot weather and warm low-water conditions will sometimes bring them out earlier.

Trout streams with mud banks, long glassy pools, or slow-moving stretches that contain ooze, muddy holes, and silt are the Green Drake's domain.

With the approach of summer the water level will be much lower than it was a month previous, and the rocks will show their tops where before they were well hidden. Large areas that were two feet deep at normal spring-water height will have become warm, quiet shallows. These are the areas that most anglers bypass as barren, but it is here that the burrowing mayfly nymphs live and where the trout are prone to feed on them.

A sudden summer squall with its rush of high water will dislodge and wash numbers of these nymphs into the waters of midstream, and in such a case the hungry trout will take these larger nymphs and fall for their imitation if fished dead drift in the main feeding lanes.

Fishing the Green Drake nymph in the late afternoon in quiet water is one of the most interesting and productive forms of nymph fishing. It is quiet-water fishing, demanding a careful approach and a well-nigh perfect delivery with a minimum of surface disturbance.

Take a position upstream from the fishing area, throw a long line, placing the nymph in the moving water and guiding it slowly into the pockets and still sections. Keep the rod tip down and move it very slowly, so as not to attract attention. Above all, do not wade any more than necessary, and refrain from lifting the line off the water until the artificial has gone well away from the area you are fishing.

Being a burrower, this nymph is somewhat active in its movements along or near the bottom, so it is advisable to occasionally give the lure a little motion with the rod tip, raising it to the surface and letting it fall again, repeating this as you work it back upstream for a fresh cast.

When the nymphs are preparing to hatch they move up toward the surface with a certain amount of kicking and a semiswimming motion. Some will hatch in the still water, though in the presence of a current they are more likely to climb onto the mud, rocks, or a snag to shed their shuck. Keep your eye on the stream for the sudden appearance of the tan-and-greenish duns, and if they are in evidence you will know that the Green Drake nymph can be fished on or near the surface as the hatch proceeds. Often when you see the trout bulging the surface among the floating duns, you can safely assume that the nymphs are on their way up.

The Green Drake found hatching on rocks near moving waters are easily recognized and interesting to watch.

While angling with me one day, my wife discovered a small group of them, and rather than fish, she preferred to watch as they went through their motions of first crawling out on the rocks, then flexing their bodies and legs until the shells split down the back. The wings then unfolded and were tenderly and carefully worked out as the insects writhed their upper bodies free. Gradually, the wings slanted upright, and after a few trial flexes the duns walked a bit, then flew a few feet away to land on the water. A trout flashed upward, grabbed one of them and was away with a splash that caused Helen to reach for her fly rod again.

On streams where conditions are favorable, these drakes are known to hatch in terrific numbers. I have seen times when the air was so filled with them that the banks of the stream were almost invisible.

The Green Drake hatch is known as "the mayfly hatch" on New York streams such as the Beaverkill, Schoharie, and lower Ausable; New Jersey streams such as the Raritan; Pennsylvania streams such as the Broadhead and Fishing Creek; and the large Michigan rivers. When anglers say "the mayflies are out," they are generally speaking of big Green Drakes.

The duns live for three or four days, and this fact is greatly appreciated by the dry-fly anglers. The transformation takes place in the early evening, and the spinner, commonly known as the Coffin Fly, will be seen over the water. Its color is entirely different from the tan-brown appearance of the dun, for it has a whitish body with slate or gray-black wings. Pretty and succulent-looking as they are, they offer little food value and consequently are not of much interest to the trout unless they are the only insects on the water or are in sufficient quantity to warrant attention—a rare occurrence.

When angling with the big dry flies, have no fear of

vodka-clear water. However, it is advisable in this quiet water to fish upstream and throw a long line.

When the Green Drakes first appear on the stream, the dry-fly anglers work their lines over the smooth runs, and explosive rises from big fish cause the excitement we all crave. This occurs when the dry-fly conditions are perfect, and that situation is not frequent on any stream, for fishing pressure is now apt to be at its height, and many of the quieter stretches of water are continually disturbed by careless wading and sloppy casting. This need not disturb the careful nymph fisherman, however.

Light Cahill

Order: *Ephemeroptera*
Family: *Heptageniidae*
Genus: *Stenonema*
Species: *ithaca, canadense,* and several others appearing together or in various localities
Nymph Type: Clinger
Nymph Size: Body: ½ in. Tails: three, ½ in.
Nymph Shape: Flat, short, and wide
Nymph Color: Body: dusty light tan. Legs: dusty buff. Wing pads: dusty gray. Tails: dirty buff
Habitat: Fast water and heads of pools

Nymph Imitation (Sens)

Hook: Size 12 Mustad Viking 94840
Silk: Primrose yellow
Tail: Three wisps of mandarin flank feather fibers (half body length)

Body: Mixture of cream-tan fur with touch of yellow wool worked in (spin loosely)
Hackle: Cream tan or pale ginger, two turns (clip off top fibers)
Wing Pads: Pearl-gray mallard flank feather (clip to shape)
Finish: Whip and varnish
Emergence: June 1 to July 15, varying according to locality, with some species hatching into July (and sometimes, in the case of small species, August). Late afternoon until dark
Dun Size: Body: ⅜ in. Wings: ½ in. Tails: two, ½ in.
Dun Color: Body: cream buff. Wings: cream dusty (yellowish milky). Legs: light tan
Standard Dun Patterns: Light Cahill, Cream Bivisible, Red Fox, Ginger Quill. Sizes 12 to 14

Nature has decreed that this fly does not hatch during the hot time of the day but rather in the late afternoon or at twilight. From midafternoon on is the time to drift the Cahill nymphs.

Fortunately for the angler, the Cahill pattern imitates several of the mayflies that hatch at the same time, so perhaps this is the reason the Light Cahill fly pattern is such a favorite in streams east of the Rockies.

Yes, Dan Cahill really had something when he designed the Cahill fly, especially the Light Cahill, for he offered the answer to one of the most confusing times of the fly-fishing season. From June on, there are about ten mayflies that are well imitated by it in the dun stage. The wet pattern when fished as a nymph also closely resembles the underwater stage, and as such is a consistent killer.

The nymphs are exceedingly difficult to spot in the water during the drift, but the presence of a few duns will tip you off to the beginning of the hatch. They are easily identified by their cream-buff and light-cream pale wings. Always watch the feeding activity of the trout. When you see a rise, be sure that it is for the dun before switching to the dry fly or even a wet fly fished on the surface. You will likely see that the rises are the follow-through of the trout as they are taking the hatching nymphs.

Observation and post-mortem inspection have proved to me that the Cahill nymph imitation tied in the conventional wet-fly pattern accurately resembles the natural in the act of emerging and when fished during a hatch is very deadly.

The Light Cahill ushers in the summer weather, and is considered by most anglers in the trout-fishing belt as the first June fly of importance. Its appearance on the stream in the early evening will be accompanied by the familiar lightning bugs.

The life cycle of the Cahill fly is very similar to those of the March Brown and the Gray Fox, in that the nymph lives in the fast water and is found in almost all trout streams. There are several important facts about this fly and the manner of its presentation which are well worth remembering.

When emergence time occurs, the nymph migrates downstream with the current to a semiquiet stretch near the head of a large deep pool. In the case of a long shallow pool the emergence takes place in the fanned-out edges.

Select a run, preferably near the head of a pool, and cast the nymph in the fringe of the main current, letting it work into quieter parts. Use a short line, and as previously mentioned, it is imperative in this type of presentation that you lift the rod tip up as the leader falls across the fast water in order to avoid line drag.

When the lure reaches the quiet water, hold the rod parallel to the surface until the line straightens. Follow

through on the swing into the side eddies, and do not retrieve until the cast is well out of the primary fishing area.
At this season of clearer water the trout are wary and easy
to put down, hence the extra word of caution.

Little Marryat (Pale Evening Dun)

Order: *Ephemeroptera*
Family: *Ephemerellidae*
Genus: *Ephemerella*
Species: *dorothea*
Nymph Type: Clamberer
Nymph Size: Body: ¼ in. Tails: three, 3/16 in.
Nymph Shape: Moderately round
Nymph Color: Body: dirty cream to tan. Legs: tan-gray
with a yellow cast. Wing pads: dark tan-gray. Tails:
three—gray-tan
Habitat: Fastest water of the aerated streams (rapidly
boiling sections), small clear brooks

Nymph Imitation (Sens)

Hook: Size 14 Mustad Viking 94836
Silk: Primrose yellow
Tail: Three mandarin flank feather fibers (just the tips)
Body: Cream-tan fur with a touch of yellow wool worked
in
Hackle: Cream to pale ginger, two turns of short hackle
(cut off top fibers)
Wing Pads: Pearl-gray mallard flank feather (clip to
shape)
Finish: Whip and varnish
Emergence: June 10 to July 10 (sometimes July 20 in
Northern streams or during high water or cold weather).
Twilight until dark

Dun Size: Body: ¼ in. Wings: ¼ in. Tails: ¼ in.
Dun Color: Body: medium tan. Legs: tan. Wings: cream.
Tails: light tan
Standard Dun Patterns: Pale Evening Dun (light smoky
wings), Sulphur Dun, Little Marryat. Sizes 14 or 16

This is strictly small-fly fishing. The nymph is barely a
quarter of an inch long and the dun likewise. The only
specimens of this nymph I have ever taken were removed
from the trout themselves, because while drifting in the
water they are difficult if not impossible to see or catch.

The Little Marryat emerges along with the Light Cahill,
and many times during a Cahill hatch I've seen trout that
were stuffed to the gills with these tiny nymphs, proving
that upon occasion the trout prefer them. The trout's
preference for the Little Marryat over the Light Cahill will
be especially evident when the water has been warm during
the day and the fish have congregated in the fast water that
is pocketed and aerated at the head of the pools.

Though I carry the dry-fly imitation of the Little
Marryat, I find it very difficult to follow in the semidarkness
while fishing the fast broken water and prefer to work the
nymph downstream, using a short line, allowing the fly to
drift close to the surface and giving the rocks and little runs
particular attention. Another good spot to fish the nymph is
along the stream edges where the current swirls and slashes
under an overhang, for quite often a surprise strike will
come from water of this fast type that is only a foot or so
deep.

The upper reaches of the feeder streams leading to our
large trout waters seem to have an abundance of these
hatches. When the flies are emerging, work a nymph into
the aerated water just below a falls or in the gravelly edges
of a fast, foaming run. Trout seem to be alert during this
hatch, and when the water is clear they will often be seen

boldly rushing a nymph imitation, sometimes just as you are about to take it out of the water for a recast.

I have often fished the Little Marryat at the mouth of one of these feeder streams when the Cahills were also hatching out in the big river and found the trout would leave them in preference for this tasty Marryat morsel. Toward dark when it is all but impossible to see the lure or the leader, the mere presence of the Little Marryat imitation in the fast water seems to take big fish. Work with a short line, and keep the imitation moving on or near the surface in the most rapidly moving stretches. Retain a supply of spare line in the left hand, for the strike will be vigorous, and the extra line acts as a shock absorber.

Brown Drake or Leadwing Coachman

Order: *Ephemeroptera*
Family: *Baetidae*
Genus: *Isonychia*
Species: *bicolor*
Nymph Type: Swimming or free-ranging type
Nymph Size: Body: ⅝ in. Tails: three, ½ in.
Nymph Shape: Oval-round and streamlined
Nymph Color: Body: dark rusty brown. Legs: dark rust. Wing pads: dark brownish black. Tails: dark rust brown
Habitat: Broad-water flats with rocks and holes

Nymph Imitation (Sens)

Hook: Size 12, 3X long
Silk: Rust
Tail: Two tiny dark rusty-brown webby hacklelike tips (only one fiber is used for less bulk)
Body: Thick bronze peacock herl ribbed counterclockwise with fine black silk to secure

Hackle: Dark rusty brown (mahogany), two turns only (clip off top fibers)
Wing Pads: Small dark brown, black-duck upper-wing covert feather (cut to shape)
Finish: Whip and varnish
Emergence: May 20 to September 20. New York, Pennsylvania, Michigan. Dusk till dark (earlier on cool dark day)
Dun Size: Body: ⅝ in. Wing: 11/16 in. 3 Tails: ½ in.
Dun Color: Body: dark tan. Legs: buff yellow to amber. Wing: dark gray-green. Tails: buff
Standard Dun Patterns: Brown Drake, Brown Quill, Mallard Quill, Leadwing Coachman. Sizes 10 and 12

This nymph is of the swimming or free-ranging type and is the most active of all the mayfly nymphs. During its entire underwater period prior to hatching it is a constant food source for the trout. Fishing the imitation is far different from that of any of the other types of nymphs, as it brings into play the "escaping form of life" technique of manipulated action.

June is their most active period, and in the late afternoon they can be seen swimming to shore or to rocks located in the streams. These nymphs are a familiar sight all lined up on a rock in various stages of transformation. They seem to have a particular habit of selecting a certain rock on which great numbers of them will congregate to cast their shucks. Strangely enough, other rocks in the neighborhood will be completely devoid of them. When this congested hatching occurs on a large midstream rock, you will usually see a great deal of trout action in the vicinity. Many times I have seen the trout jump clear out of water to land well up on a rock and slither back down again, in pursuit of the elusive Leadwing nymph. Brown trout, especially, assume a voracious feeding and chasing activity during this hatch.

I have had my best results in fishing the nymph imitation or the Leadwing Coachman wet-fly pattern at twilight when coolness has developed in the air and shadows are darkening the stream edges. It is primarily fishing downstream and across at a 45-degree angle. Let the fly work well down through the faster midstream water, and during this first part of its travels it is unnecessary to impart action to any degree. When the fly swings out of the run into the side water, treat it as a miniature bucktail, giving it a series of short quick pulls, pausing to let it sink down and finally resuming action as before. Let it break the surface occasionally, and if you are using a long line, take advantage of the distance and permit the cast to work into the shallows and among the shoreline rocks. This swing towards the shore seems to simulate the nymph en route to the hatching rock. Many times I have experienced savage rushes and slashes at the fly in water scarcely deep enough to cover the fish.

One way of drawing the attention of the bigger fish in midstream is to drag the fly on the surface for a few seconds, pause to let it sink down deep, and then resume the short, swimming, gliding, or darting motion.

I recall one particular trout that had been a constant irritant to several of us who had tried in vain to take him all season long. After a council of war one day, it was decided that we would try a spinning lure and attempt to snag the old fellow. We talked far into the night about this dragon fish and of our various unsuccessful attempts upon his life. It was only after looking at my records of emergence dates that Zeke got the idea of going after him with a Leadwing nymph.

"Boys," he said, "hold off on the spinning tackle for one more day, I think I have the answer to this problem. I've got a nymph that might just appeal to the old devil and the time is ripe to use it."

Late next afternoon, Zeke and I walked down along the bank to a place opposite the rock, and sure enough there were a few of the nymphs crawling out. We stood for many minutes while several insects dragged themselves aboard. When we saw the slap of a tail and a definite swirl, we knew the big boy was actively on the feed, evidently taking the nymphs as they approached the rock.

Carefully Zeke waded well upstream from the location, and after the surface water had resumed its twilight calm, cast directly down, stopping the lure in midair to drop it quietly in the water ten feet above the rock. Letting it drift to what he gauged to be a couple of feet away, he began gently dragging the line, being careful not to overdo it. Several times he let the nymph settle back to drift even closer, meanwhile holding his breath for fear the hook would snag on the rock. Slowly Zeke raised the nymph, and at just the point when it broke the surface the old dog wanted it and in much less time than it takes to tell he had the nymph and was well on his way to wrapping the leader around any snag he could find. The battle was one of desperate attempts to keep the trout up from the bottom and at the same time stop the mad dashes on the surface. I heard voices behind me, and the Folkert boys along with Ernie and Paul waded out to Zeke to watch the fun.

When the trout came close to the net Zeke took hold of the leader and said, "Okay boys, it's your turn—I'm going to let him go and see who catches him next."

Giant Stone Fly

Order: *Plecoptera*
Family: *Pteronarcidae*
Genus: *Pteronarcys*
Species: *dorsata*
Coloration: Light mottled brown, gray and black

Size: Over-all length: 1¼ in. to 1½ in.
Habitat: Medium-fast sections of streams
Emergence: June to September. New York, Pennsylvania, Michigan, Montana, Oregon

ADULT IMITATION (Sens)

Hook: Size 4, 3X long
Silk: Brown
Tail: Mottled turkey-feather section
Body: Rabbit hair tied thick with guard hairs extending out. Rib with yellow yarn
Hackle: Rusty dun (long)
Wings: Mottled turkey-wing feather fibers tied double, tent-shaped over body (rather than flat)
Finish: Whip and varnish

The giant stone fly is mentioned here only to cover the subject of night fishing, for this type of stone fly is a night flier and night hatcher. Night-fishing success requires that you know the particular stretch of stream that you will fish after dark. Never attempt strange water in the black of night or you are liable to break an ankle or fall into a hole. When certain runs are known well by daylight, a course can easily be plotted that will lessen the chance of accidents and will also help you to fish the water properly.

To appreciate why night fishing is so productive and fascinating, the angler need only consider the stream conditions that bring about this nocturnal sport with large trout, trout that can seldom if ever be taken before the sun has set and the shroud of darkness has descended over the river. It is the magic time that transforms the stream.

The best night fishing is reserved by nature for summer

and late season angling when the days are hot and the water low and clear. It is then that the trout hide under rocks, rock ledges, or in deep holes behind stream obstructions.

The large trout sleep out the day in a semidormant state and following the adage of "mad dogs and Englishmen," stay well hidden from the sun and light, awaiting the descent of darkness before foraging for food.

Their hiding ability is amazing, for during these bright days, every nook and cranny, every inch of the stream bottom is blatantly visible. Much scrutiny, however, will seldom reveal the form of a large trout. The angler who fishes these torrid days will raise only the brash little ones.

One wonders where the fish go to reappear seemingly from nowhere after the sun has set and the coolness steals over the stream. It was during one of my trips to the Neversink that I had a chance to observe the daytime habits of warm-weather trout.

One hot August afternoon I was ambling along the shady bank and chanced to spot a good-sized brown lying close in behind a big boulder. Had the surface reflections not parted at the precise moment of my glance, I'd never have seen him. Coming closer to the stream edge, I watched him for several minutes. The sun was glaring down, and its hot rays seemed to penetrate the cool Neversink waters, for even the submerged rocks and gravel looked hot. The brown was wrapped around the lee side of the rock, and his body was just inside the shade mark. He hardly moved a fin, and his gills opened just enough to let in oxygen to keep him alive.

His spots and marking were plainly visible. Boy, what a trout! I picked up a pebble and threw it into the water above his head, and though it fell within a few inches of his nose he showed no interest. After repeated trials, I quietly touched him on the tail with a tree branch. That awakened him and he dashed into the center of the pool. Certainly a trout that sleepy would be hard to entice with any method of daytime angling.

I recall another trout I discovered while peering into the water from a somewhat precarious position on a long rock ledge. I dangled a nice juicy worm in front of his nose and breathlessly awaited the jarring strike, but none came, even after repeated offerings of the choice meal. By accident my foot slipped into the water, and the trout woke up in a hurry, saw the worm, grabbed it smartly, and was off with a terrific rush into the pool. I realized then why it is so difficult to interest trout during the day in hot weather. This fellow, too, had been asleep.

Had it not been that Jack was two hours late in picking me up on the stream, it might have been years before I would have put these discoveries to work. Jack had taken the car upstream and was to meet me at sundown at the Bridge Pool, and rather than go ashore, I decided to keep fishing until he arrived.

There were no signs of him, however, and darkness descended, and it was all I could do to make out the position of the fly when it hit the water. The outlines of the rocks on the far side of the stream were barely visible and even the sky was dark, for the haze and clouds covered any faint light the stars would have given.

Casting was more or less a guessing game of distance and location, and I was sure I was wasting my time. I wondered if Jack had had an accident or a flat tire or had passed me and was looking for me downstream. Out there in the dark the imagination can conjure up many visions.

It was no vision, however, when I heard and felt an explosion. Instinctively I struck, and it was like snagging a stone. But the stone turned out to be something wild, big, and fast-moving. The throb of the rod handle was like that usually experienced only in salmon fishing. The trout ran down into the body of the run, taking line directly from the reel.

Suddenly a beam of light creased the pool's surface.

"Jack," I yelled. "I've got a monster on out here . . . where the hell have you been?"

"Never mind that . . . hold him, brother . . . I'll be there in a minute."

It seemed like hours before Jack reached my side. He had had to climb back into his waders. When the monster brown was netted, his first remark was, "For a fish like that I'll gladly walk three miles for a wrench and change a tire to boot."

"Next week when we come up here we fish this water at sundown and dark, not sunup and during the day." I said.

To say that night fishing can be thrilling is a masterpiece of understatement. Certainly it is different in all respects from any other form of taking trout. It is made up of strange sounds in the silence—even the whish of the cast in the air is echoed in the trees. It has a quietude and yet is crammed with the anticipation of impending action that can happen at any moment—at the drop, during the drift, or on the retrieve. The stream seems to swallow all noises heard in the daytime, but night sounds issue eerie crackings in the trees, rustles in the underbrush, wet sounds as the fly spats the surface on the cast. Distance is no more, the opposite bank has no definition, and unless the confines of the pool are well known from previous observation it might be two hundred feet away or barely thirty. Even the length of line cannot be determined other than by timing the false casts. Wading need not be a problem on familiar water, but because sight is restricted, more care and caution is exercised. It is like walking through the rooms of your house in the dark. Though you might know them well, the blackness can be quite confusing.

Lest there be any doubt about the sporting angle of night fishing, I'll go on record to say that this method of taking trout is no less sporting than any other. Method does not take fish from the stream—it is the angler. And there is no law against returning hooked fish to the stream, either day or night.

Don't get the idea that night fishing is easy. It is not. There is a lot to the approach, presentation, and other aspects of night fishing that if not thoroughly observed will leave the fisherman tired and fishless.

Briefly stated, it is best to know your water well from previous daytime observation, noting the snags, overhanging trees, deep holes, and best casting angles. Also mark well the paths to be taken to and from the water, for the flashlight is used only on the return trip, never turned on when you are within fifty yards of the stream. Cigarette smokers will have to wait until the fishing is over, for no light of any description can be on the water.

Fish only one man to a pool, and make the entrance inches at a time, following all the cautions of daytime angling. Cause no ripples, and avoid scraping or rolling of stones or crunching of gravel. Unless the approach is virtually noiseless, the trip will be useless if you want to catch the big ones.

When you have waded to the spot where you will begin to cast, wait at least three minutes, standing perfectly still. This will offer time to acquire an eye for the darkness and a "look" at the surroundings.

Make only short casts, at the most thirty feet, as there is little need for spot casting. The fish will be on the roam and might be picked up anywhere on the water. Keep just enough tension on the line to maintain contact with the fly. Pause between casts, and don't work the same area in successive casts. If a fish rises and misses, count to sixty, slowly, before recasting. Move along by inches to a new position and only then resume casting after the waiting period.

It is advisable to select a spot where the stream current suddenly slows down into a deep hole, an area often located at the end of a reef-like stretch in the center of the pool. These places will be particularly potent if large boulders and snags are along either bank, for these are the hiding places of the big trout, and it is from here they venture when the protective darkness has fallen over the stream.

With this spot prestudied and your movements preplanned, start fishing at about the time the first bats appear. Proceed slowly, and if you wade and are wearing chains, do not scuff your feet unnecessarily, because big fish are much more easily disturbed by sound than by sight. Armed with a leader tapered down to about 9/5 and the Giant Stone Fly, cast a short line on a 45-degree angle across and downstream, laying as straight and free a line as possible to avoid missing any immediate strike. Let me say here that the moment the fly touches the water is one of the most important times, since a feeding trout nearby will seldom think twice if he sees the lure. He will often grab the fly before you have become organized.

Let the current do all the work, and as soon as the line drifts downstream the rod is held four or six inches off the surface and pointed directly at the line. This is also done so that a strike will be instantly felt, and when it is, all you have to do is to raise the rod tip sharply. Do not strike until you actually feel the pull on the line. If you strike at the sound of action, you are liable to take the fly away from the trout before he closes his mouth on it.

I followed the above advice one cool evening, and after making a couple of casts into the dark I knew the stretch contained big trout. I heard a short sucking sound and felt a slight hit. Evidently the fish missed the fly. After resting the area a minute or so before recasting, I cast again, trying vainly to make out some form in the water. Again there came the sound of a large trout breaking the surface. Resting the area once more, I cast well upstream and let the lure drift to the approximate location of the sound. The current acted on the line just enough to tighten it, and I looked for a sign of the fish and hoped that he'd take it more definitely this time.

There was a slap like that of a log falling into the water and instantly my rod felt as if someone had sneaked up in the dark to grab it from me. The bend of the shivering bamboo was felt right down to the cork grip, and when a trout makes you feel that way—brother, it is a big one. I was literally pulled in over my boot tops, something I'd thought could be caused only by an Atlantic salmon. When the fish did swim in close I could see a faint shimmer along his length. Believe me, from then on, I handled him gingerly until he was on his side. The fight was a long one, and netting was a simple matter because I had practically killed the fish before attempting to bring him in.

Yes, try, night fishing if you tire of little fish. You are in for some thrills.

I might interject that in making the study of the insects, the trout, and the cycle, it has never been my intention to take ruthlessly all the fish from the stream. When you become acquainted with nature to the extent of recognizing at least a few basic secrets of the stream, the whole meaning of angling becomes an entirely different concept. Sure, it is fun to click when the other fellow can't. It is gratifying when you can call your shots and take fish in enough quantity that the tab can't be classified as luck. It is also nice to be able to lug home a lunker for supper once in a while, knowing that you were able to fit the picture puzzle of the stream together and virtually call him into the net. Several angling friends have told me that what I have written here is an exposé on Mother Nature and that I shouldn't put it in black and white, because too many fish might be taken because of it. Well, my answer is that when a man can perform this well, he has graduated, if you will, well beyond the stage of wanting to take fish home in quantity. He enjoys all the aspects of his days on·the water—the exciting story of the streamside drama, the glimpse beneath the surface, and the inside story of the private lives of trout and their habits. I know that if we had all taken and released as many trout as Ed Sens has, we would all have become the most fanatical of conservationists. The net results of Ed's days astream have never been weighed by pounds of dead fish but by the highest pleasures of angling.

The patterns described in the foregoing chapter were all designed by Ed Sens in the late 1940s. Over the years they've taken trout readily when conditions have called for them. It would seem, then, that no more nymph patterns would be necessary to carry astream. Perhaps this is really so. But, again, the creativity and desires of the angler change, and so have some of these patterns changed as I've enlarged my scope of angling and have spent more time in the West.

Below is a series of nymph and wet-fly patterns that I choose to call augmentations on the originals. They are presented as the current evolution of the original Sens patterns.

Fishing the Film

The film of water on the very surface is perhaps the most potent level of water from the bottom to the dry-fly top. Here a certain magnetism collects insects and drifting material from blow-ins as well as up from the water below. This attraction brings to the film all of the insects that are drifting down the current, be they dead flies, blow-ins, or hatched aquatics and, at hatching time, the nymphs that are casting their shucks and breaking out as sub adults (in the case of mayflies) or adults (in the case of caddis and stone flies). Actually, the mayflies that are about to hatch may drift in the lower currents for a while after leaving the bottom, but the actual casting of the shuck, usually happens right in the film. The magnetic attraction of the film holds them next to the surface. If this were not so they would flounder under water, and if their wings broke out of the shell too soon, before they reach the film, their chances of flying away would be almost nil, since they would have to break the surface film to do so. Locked in, then, during the changeover, they are in a position to float on the top of the surface film when the time is right. Look closely when you encounter a hatch, and you'll see the nymph casting off the shuck and the fly struggling to become airborne. For a few seconds after the emergence the fly is right on the middle line of the surface film. When the insect starts to flex its wings, it is riding partially on the top. Follow the insect as it drifts a few feet, and you'll see it fully emerge and ride on the top of the film.

The caddis emerges a bit differently. At the instant the cellophane-like sac buoys the insect to the surface, the sac is *broken* by the film, and the insect pops right out, on the surface. There is no long drift of the fly in the film such as happens with the mayfly.

How to fish the film? One of the oldest techniques used by wet-fly fishermen is to dap the flies on the surface, using a short line. Here drag is welcomed. The hatching insects make a good deal of commotion in the film. The skittering technique on the down-and-across-stream drift breaks the surface film in much the same way the live insect does. This looks good to the trout, and they take the fly mostly because of this action. Almost any pattern close in size to the hatching insect will connect. Since this action is in the broken film, not much color can be detected by the trout, and so they are not very selective. Nymphs fished under the film can be more readily seen, and it is then that the trout can be most selective.

Fishing the film also involves fishing the nymph as a dry fly and the dry fly as a partially sunken fly. Take a soft-hackled dry fly that allows the body of the fly to be partially submerged in the film. This represents the emerging dun. Take a nymph, dope it to float, and you have virtually the same thing—an insect imitation stuck in the surface film and breaking the film with sparkles of refracted light.

The high-floating dry fly, on the other hand, represents the hatched insect, riding high on the water with only a small part of its body breaking the surface film. Quite often neither the natural nor artificial is seen by the trout, since their attention is on the film or on the water directly under it. The dry fly sometimes fails not because of pattern or size but because it is riding *above* the surface film. Sink that dry fly down *into the film* and you have something special.

The same is true of big wet flies and streamers. Break that surface film and the reflections will attract trout from all quarters. When the fly is fished even two inches below the film the trout have time to look it over. That's why the streamer dappled and pulled erratically on the surface can be twice as killing as one fished a foot or so under.

CHAPTER IV

It's Fun to Tie Flies

It's great fun to tie your own flies. You become part inventor, part artist-craftsman, and there is a particular thrill of anticipation as you see in your mind's eye your creation, no matter how humble or how perfect, being gobbled up by a hungry trout!

Fly tying is a "Duke's Mixture" of practical trout lore and a smattering of entomology. The ingredients include varicolored feathers, a conglomeration of fur, tinsel, yarn, quills, and wire, topped off with a generous portion of imagination and creative ability.

Like good chefs, fly tiers combine famous recipes with their own ad-libs. The trout has to exert the utmost caution when he dines if he is to avoid falling for an imitation of his succulent numph cocktail, his flavorsome and filling entree of minnows, or his tasty dessert of a fast mayfly or two. Yes, it is a very clever trout that can tell the well-made imitation from the real thing.

Since the days of Thaddeus Norris and Theodore Gordon, interest in angling has zoomed from a handful of anglers to

an enthusiastic army of over twenty-five million in this country and, quite naturally, interest in fly tying has grown accordingly. One well-known fly-tying manufacturer employs over three hundred people in his plant and does a gross business of over two million dollars a year. There are hundreds of individual comercial tiers averaging an income of between three and five thousand dollars a year, and many of these have become famous, not only in their own fishing locales but nationally as well.

During the Sportsmen's Show in New York, I was very fortunate in having the annual opportunity to learn of the tremendous interest there is in fly tying. One of my business acquaintances had been introducing a revolutionary type of fly-tying vise and asked if I could help him out as a demonstrator during the lunch hour or in the evening. I consented not only because I wanted to see just what kind of an interest fly tying had for the general public that attended the show, but also because I was eager to pick up any hints from the amateur and professional tiers that chanced to stop by the booth. In demonstrating the vise, it was of course necessary to tie many flies, and though our booth was small, there was scarcely a minute when there wasn't at least thirty people watching. Some would sit down and tie, others would crowd around and watch the procedure completely fascinated. One point that impressed me was the fact that so many of the anglers said something to this effect: "I have always wanted to tie my own flies, but it seemed like a difficult job." Their problems and questions were similar to mine before I discovered just how easy fly tying could be. It was only after a very close angling friend had me sit down with him one evening to watch and later try my own hand that I tied my first fly and the virus took hold!

We all need encouragement to start in, but many of us do not have the urging friend or the opportunity to see a professional at work. If I can intrigue you into getting started with the simplified instructions to come, I am sure that you too will become an ardent fan. To my mind, fly tying rounds out the word "complete" when it comes to the enjoyment of angling. Not that it is impossible to derive heaps of satisfaction when fishing with "bought-en" ones, but there is a great sense of achievement when you "roll your own." You will find, too, that the study of the Cycle of the Season can bring tangible results at the fly vise, even though you may continue to buy some flies.

Patterns

Years ago, when only a few standard patterns were commonly used, it was much simpler for the trout to recognize and remember them. The art of fly tying was practiced by only a few, and these men and women supplied practically all of the artificial flies and lures that were available. Today, however, the standard patterns have increased by leaps and bounds, not to mention the numerous original creations of Tom, Dick, and Harry of our angling fraternity.

The angler who believes in the imitation school has a clear and unlimited field of experimentation ahead of him, for certainly there is a lot of room for the perfection of natural nymph, wet-fly, and streamer patterns. Dry flies too can be developed for individual situations and requirements.

Fly tying in the off season offers many hours of interest and relaxation, not to mention the opportunity of applying the knowledge gained from days spent on the stream the season previous. Fly tying "on the spot"—the selecting of an insect from the water and duplicating it right then and there--is an exciting experience, especially when the new creation catches a fish!

Many of the traditional patterns have quite a story. The Red Hackle, one of the most famous of all time, dates back to antiquity. The Beaverkill fly was first tied about 1850 by Harry Pritchard, an American. He patterned it after an English fly and named it after his favorite stream, the Beaverkill in Sullivan County, New York. The Bivisible family of flies originated by Edward R. Hewitt was designed for use on the Neversink. The Gray or Leadwing Coachman was created by an Englishman, Henry R. Francis, around 1850, but Tom Bosworth, who served King George IV of England and William IV and Queen Victoria as coachman, was the originator of the Coachman fly. The Quill Gordon was the product of Theodore Gordon, tier of the first American dry flies. If you can, get a copy of Gordon's life story. It is a book steeped in traditional trout lore and the early angling history of fly-fishing for trout in America. Every time I use the Quill Gordon I can't help but think of the romance behind this drab-looking creation, designed by one of the most famous men in American angling history and literature. He tied flies for A.E. Hendrickson of Scarsdale, New York, for whom the Hendrickson pattern was designed and named by its inventor, Roy Steenrod. The Parmachene Belle was first tied by Henry P. Wells in 1878 and named after Parmachene Lake in Maine. This fly was supposed to imitate the fin of a brook trout. There are thousands of fly patterns, each bearing its own story.

Today, in an age of thousands of fly tiers, millions of fishermen, and a growing multimillion-dollar market for the manufacturers and dealers, there is a constant demand for any new type of lure. Its success depends in large measure on how it is launched, usually with an article in a sporting magazine proclaiming it "a sure-fire killer," with subsequent follow-up publicity where it is sold in the tackle shop. This is a great business and a lot of fun for the angler who reads the magazines and in the off season wanders into his tackle store just itching to buy something. Today, as always, many lures on the market are made to catch fishermen, not that it can be said that these lures will not catch fish. There is no lure ever invented that will not catch fish if used long and hard enough, even though its design may not be basic.

In fishing many regions of the United States and Canada, I have always made it a practice to go to a local tier or tackle shop for information about the streams in the immediate vicinity and the flies that the fish are taking. When you take the natives' advice and fish any one of the recommended lures consistently, you are likely to connect.

The flies in your collection become mementos, and each bears a story and a memory. My father presented me with a fly the other day that I had not seen for some twenty-odd years. It is a small salmon streamer fly that was responsible for the first big trout I caught in New Brunswick. Another I prize highly is a battered McGinty that a guide in Yosemite sold me while on a trip to one of the high Sierra lakes.

Fly-Tying Equipment

Here's a good rule to follow when you are involved in a hobby that requires tools—always buy the best, have all the necessary equipment, and use it for what it was designed. There are few tools necessary in all but commercial or assembly-line fly production.

You'll need a solid table with an edge that will accommodate a clamp-on vise. Good close light should be over the vise, shining on the work, not in your eyes. The vise, your most important piece of equipment, must be sturdy and designed to hold the hook securely and allow "elbow room" for your hands and fingers. Hackle pliers, especially designed to hold the delicate feathers, are a necessity. A sharp pair of narrow-bladed scissors is essential.

It is advisable to keep your materials in order, and the manner in which you do this depends largely on the amount of material you keep. Feathers can be kept in ordinary labeled business envelopes or discarded shoe boxes. Or you may wish to buy a cabinet specially designed for this purpose. There are various sizes of fiber or metal-drawer cabinets on the market. These should be mothproofed.

Fly-Tying Vise

There are a number of fly-tying vises available on the market today, ranging in price from a few dollars to fifteen dollars or more. The one I recommend and use for the basis of instruction further in the chapter is the Universal Fly Tying Vise. Thanks to the genius and inventive ability of a Massachusetts railroad mechanic, the old-fashioned method of manual winding is no longer necessary. This vise rotates the hook instead, making it possible to control the material with an even tension, so that it winds on the hook neatly and quickly. This rotary vise is as important an invention to the fly tier as was the lathe to the machinist. It can be set at any angle and used by a left- or right-handed person without shifting the tool itself. The shaft can be raised or lowered to adjust to the eye comfort of the individual.

I have witnessed demonstrations of the vise as used in occupational therapy treatment in veterans' hospitals as well as private institutions where fly tying is a wonderful new hobby for shut-ins.

Let's Tie a Fly!

Assemble your material on the table and have all equipment within easy reach. Described below is the detailed
tying operation for the standard type of wet fly. We will not
discuss any specific patterns but will concentrate only on
the tying operation. The procedure outlined is applicable to
the rotary vise, though the directions can be used with
the stationary vise as well.

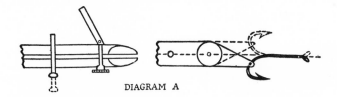

DIAGRAM A

Preparing to Tie the Fly

(1) Set up the vise as in the photograph with the chuck
bar parallel to your body and adjusted to a comfortable
working height. Adjust the bar as near level as possible so
that the hook will not wobble when revolved.

(2) Kick off the release cam which opens the vise jaws.
(Diagram A.) Insert the hook bend between the jaws with
the barb down, line up the hook as near center as possible
and close the clamp. *Always twirl the vise toward you in all
tying operations.*

Waxing the Silk

Pull the length of silk selected for tying through a small
piece of specially made fly-tying wax. The reason for using
waxed tying silk is to keep the thread from slipping during

the tying operation. The wax also makes the silk easier to handle. Prewaxed thread can be bought, and many tiers prefer it.

DIAGRAM B

Necessary Tying Knots

You must first attach the tying silk, and this is done by wrapping the silk over itself around the hook several times. (Do not tie a knot here, as it will revolve.) (Diagram B)

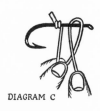

DIAGRAM C

Half-Hitch Knot

This is necessary to secure your work after many of the operations. We show here the simplest way which is also the best for all purposes. (Diagram C)

Tying the Tail

We will tie a simple type of wet fly composed of tail, body material, wings and hackle—nothing fancy, but it is the basis of all operations.

(1) Attach the tying silk (a length of at least 24 inches, unless bobbin is used) to the hook, as described above, placing it approximately in the middle of the shank. Spinning the vise toward you, roll the silk back toward the hook bend. (Diagram D) Clip off the surplus. Secure by half hitch or by dropping the bobbin. (Bobbin weight will hold the silk tight.) (Diagram E)

DIAGRAM D   DIAGRAM E

(2) Select the tail material. This may be a few of the long fibers of a feather from a hackle neck or one or two fibers from a wing feather or possibly a short tuft of yarn. For our purposes here, we'll use hackle fibers.

(3) Grasp the selected fibers between the left thumb and forefinger, butts forward, and place tightly over the hook shank just ahead of the bend. (Diagram F) Holding them tight, wrap two or three turns (Diagram G) of silk over the tail material and one turn under and one over (between tail and hook shank) to secure its position. Secure by half hitch, or drop bobbin. Clip off the surplus.

DIAGRAM F   DIAGRAM G

Tying the Body

(1) Grasp a piece of body material. This can be a short piece of yarn, floss, stripped hackle quill, chenille, tinsel, fur or other material. For our purposes here, we'll use a length of yarn four inches long. This is placed on top of the hook shank, over the bend and tail winding, butt forward. Make two or three windings and secure. (Diagram H)

DIAGRAM H   DIAGRAM I

(2) Next, wind the tying silk forward toward the eye of the hook (Diagram I) and half hitch so that the knot is on the top of the hook. When vise is spun the thread will drop

over the eye with each revolution. If bobbin is used, after material is tied in, wind several wide loops forward and place bobbin over bobbin rest.

(3) Now, holding the body material taut in the right hand, spin the knurled stem or vise wheel toward you and guide the material forward. (It may be necessary in some patterns to wind back and forth to form a tapered or fat body.) Wrap at least three-quarters of the shank length, leaving ample room for the future operations of the hackle, wings, and head of the fly. Keep tension on body material and slide back the half hitch, wrap several turns and secure. When using the bobbin, pick bobbin off its rest and tie in material as usual, then let bobbin hang.

If the pattern calls for more than one color or type of material for ribbing, such as tinsel, wire or the like, tie both pieces of material in at the same time. Wrap the tying silk forward as described, spin on the main body material first and secure by cross wrapping and cutting off the surplus. Half hitch or rest the tying silk (bobbin) over the bobbin rest and then grasp the ribbing material and spin it on forward in evenly spaced revolutions for neat appearance and then cross wrap with the tying silk to secure. (A pattern example of ribbing is Sens March Brown or Gray Fox nymph.) In the case of tinsel bodies for streamer flies, tie in the tinsel near the head of the fly, wrap back to the hook bend and again forward and tie off. This makes for a uniform job.

NOTE: The revolving vise makes it much simpler to tie bodies, and you will find that it is not only faster but easier and that a much better job will be done, especially by the beginner, for an even tension of the material is easier to maintain. Also, you don't have any twist put in the material which occurs in any manual winding. Another advantage is that you are able to view your work from any angle, or turn the fly when clipping or adjusting feathers.

Spun Fur Bodies

The simplest way to make these is to select the desired color from a piece of skin, using the under fur or soft dubbing. Pull this out and eliminate the stiff outer guard hairs. Have your tying silk well waxed and held in the left hand. In the right hand, hold the loose fur in a narrow, partially rolled length—just enough to hold it together. Place it on the tying silk and roll on by twisting the silk, maintaining tension with the left hand. Slowly revolve the vise and lead the material forward just as you did with the yarn.

Tying the Hackle

There are several ways of hackling wet flies. The simplest is to strip off a small bunch of fibers from a hackle feather and tie them in on the underside of the hook just behind the eye (just ahead of the body) (Diagram J). With the revolving vise this is simple, for all you do is make a half turn of the wheel and the bottom side of the hook is now up. Apply the same technique as you did in tying in the tail feathers.

DIAGRAM J

Tying the Wings

Select wing material (for instance, sections of matched duck-quill flight feathers), placing them with inside curves together. Grasp the wing material tightly in the left thumb and forefinger, placing it butt first on top of the hook shank just forward of the body windings (directly above the hackle). Wrap the tying silk over the butt ends by bringing it up tightly and then down *between the tightly closed fingers* (Diagram K) and over the material. This is done to

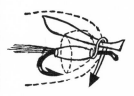

DIAGRAM K

keep wings firm and firmly on top of the hook, until secured
in place for good. Repeat for two or three windings,
remembering to hold the material vertical and tight
throughout the operation. Half hitch and cut off the butt
surplus. The tying operation for the Sens patterns of nymph
are as outlined here for tying the wet fly with the exception
of the wing-pad feather. (Cut to shape to represent the
nymphal shape of the wing pad of the nymph.) Cut
prescribed feather to shape (Diagram L) and tie in flat on
the top of the body.

DIAGRAM L

Tying the Head of the Fly

Spin tying silk to shape fly head, half hitch several times
and varnish or lacquer.

Tying Nymphs

Though many individuals have named their nymph
creations, there is, as yet, no standardization of patterns. Ed
Sens chooses, for instance, to use the same names as the
accepted standard wet-fly and dry-fly patterns, as they too
are used to imitate the winged form of the insects described
in the Cycle of the Season section. Imitating the nymphal
life of our streams is relatively new, and since fly tying now
is a hobby of millions of anglers, it is very unlikely that a
standard set will be adopted until the individuals or commercial concerns band together and standardize them, the
same as they have done with the American fly patterns and
those English standards which have been adapted to our
fishing.

The nymph imitations that Ed Sens has given us in the
Cycle of the Season are in this writer's opinion a very good
start as a complete set of the necessary types. There are

bound to be regional variances. However the Sens nymphs are as near an exact imitation of the naturals as is required for the most common well-distributed insect species.

The actual tying operation of the nymph requires the basic steps which are standard fly-tying procedure. The only difference is that more operations are necessary in applying the materials and working out the desired effects. One suggestion Ed advances is to be sure that the colors you pick for the nymph materials appear as you want them when wet, and in selecting material for the color scheme it is advisable to wet a short length and check its color.

There are on the market many "exact imitations" of nymphs. These are mostly hard-bodied and include hard life-like legs. I believe that exact imitation to this extent is unnecessary, for if you were to watch a nymph closely and observe its actions in the water, you would see at a glance that action is as important as actual shape. The nymph patterns that are listed in the Cycle of the Season are far from "exact" imitations if you carefully compare them with their natural counterparts. They do however convey an impression, once they are in the water, of a live nymph. Nymph bodies do not necessarily need to be flat to be effective. Those tied with fur that is picked out generously are made to represent the body of the nymph and the many active gills of the insect. The hackles, or legs, are few in number and not very large, again to simulate movement rather than to imitate exactly. Color and over-all size are very important. Study the nymphs found in your stream, and blend your colors carefully.

Starting Patterns

I suggest that the beginner at fly tying should select easy patterns to start with and master the tying of a perfect fly

in simple patterns before progressing on to the more involved fly types and patterns. Once the basic principles
have been fairly well mastered, the more involved flies can
then be attempted. For one thing, a very few hackles and
feathers and other materials are needed, but the more
patterns attempted, the more varied materials will be
required. For your own benefit, stick to standard dressings
at first. Do not start out inventing your own patterns.
Practice on the standards until you learn all about the
necessary materials and ways of tying. Only then is it a
good idea to ad-lib.

CHAPTER V
Striking, Playing and Landing

These are the three operations which constitute the most exciting moments of angling. A trout has been wooed to the artificial, and unless hooked well, played skillfully, and netted safely, all may be lost. There are times, of course, when trout hook themselves, and sometimes even the worst handling brings them to the creel; but one can never know how securely a trout is hooked until after it has been examined in the net. The hook often falls out when the fish thumps in the meshes, yet there are other times when the extraction of the barb may be difficult.

Luck enters the picture, and regardless of careful handling, everyone sometimes loses good fish. Once a big Beaverkill brown hit my nymph with power enough almost to throw me off balance. The next thing I knew he was four feet in the air, and as far as I am concerned he's still up there and still going, for all I did was to reel in a very dead line and look into blank space. There wasn't any time for either good or bad handling.

Eliminating Slack for Slow-Water Striking

Most anglers fish with too long a line and usually develop slack. When the trout takes the fly very little of the hit will be felt, and unless the take is instantly acted upon the trout can and does eject the lure. A favorite excuse among anglers is "the fish were hitting light today." Often these so-called light hits would have resulted in hooked fish had the angler been able to make a quick strike.

Quite often another answer to "light hits" can be found. An interesting experience introduced me to an entirely fresh slant on these so-called missed strikes.

I shall never forget when four of us were fishing "Rock Cut" on the Esopus, a long, wide, and smooth pool. On this particular afternoon the only way of promoting action was to drift a large dry fly constantly over the entire length of water, and sooner or later one of the big browns or rainbows would burst into the air in a smacking rise. They were hard to hook though, because of the long line we had to use in order to reach the runs where they were lying.

Paul managed to take three fish from his many rises, and my wife Helen rose two but landed only one. My score was embarrassing, for though I received hit after hit, not a single fish was played. The effect was maddening, and I tried striking fast and hard at the slightest suggestion of a rise in hope that I'd connect, "on time." When this failed to pay off I began to wonder if the fish really wanted my fly, despite the fact that they had shown enough interest in it to rise.

I decided to find out then and there, and for the next three good rises, left the fly on the water without striking at all. In all three cases the fly was never touched, despite the definite and flashy show put on by the fish. The fourth rise was equally dramatic and the fly disappeared from the surface but in a second popped back up again. That was a taking rise, and had I struck at all or at least had had no slack on the water I am certain that the fish would have hooked himself.

The next cast went well out on the pool, and very gradually I gathered in the slack until the line was almost straight from the rod tip to the fly. There was a rise, and the hit was instantly felt in the rod handle. This time the trout hooked himself as he headed down underwater.

(A) Too much slack—feed it out as fly drifts down.
(B) Correct—feed out line but still "keep in touch."

(A) Too much slack—strike will not be felt—strip in line
(B) Correct—no drag, no slack—strike will be felt

This striking action is readily seen in salmon angling, for when a twenty-pound fish comes out of water and bangs down on the fly yet does not take it, there is no mistaking his intentions. Salmon will often crash down on a fly with no thought of taking it into their mouths but in a fit of chasing or madness will be snagged by the angler's strike as the hook passes them. This is the reason salmon are sometimes hooked in the back, belly, or tail.

There is no mistaking a real honest-to-goodness "taking" rise. There is nothing short, nothing hesitant about it, whether it be salmon or trout!

All of this action happens fast and can be seen in dry-fly angling. Seldom can it be noted to any degree in wet-fly fishing, but it occurs just the same, pointing up the importance of eliminating slack line and keeping it under control all the time the fly is being fished.

A properly handled fish should never escape with the fly in his mouth. There is little excuse for breaking the leader, assuming that the fly is tied securely. A fast quick rise of a fish to a fly on a controlled line needs little initial setting in order to sink the barb, and the dash of the fish after he grabs it is normally enough to secure it permanently. With the ever-present chance that a big fish might hit, it is advisable on strike to flip the rod up or sideways, so that the spare coils of line held in the left hand can act as a cushion when needed. Some anglers strike from the reel, having set the drag to a safe tension. I do not recommend this for most small or average trout.

Remember that the big trout which takes a slowly drifting fly in quiet water seldom hits hard, so the angler must strike with just enough force to set the hook. I have observed sizable fish feeding under these conditions, and they seldom dash away after taking the real insect but seem, rather, to drop back or down to swallow the morsel. Then, and then only, is the time to tighten and then strike.

Roll-Cast Strike

When you are fishing with an exceptionally long line and there is quite a bit of slack, the conventional back hoist, even with the double haul, is generally not fast or efficient enough to reach the hook in time.

Have you ever noticed how quickly you pick up the line when you roll cast first and then haul back?

Well, next time you want a fast, efficient strike, roll ahead as if you were doing the conventional roll-cast pick-up, only do with a bit more gusto than usual. You'll hook your trout.

Fast-Water Striking

When hooking fish in fast water the problems are greatly minimized by the force of the current. For one thing, the fish are bound to take the artificial with much more gusto, a fact especially true in streamer fishing. They move fast and strike before the current has whisked the fly by them, in order to retain their upstream position, rather than head downcurrent after a fly. The line and leader are not nearly as slack, especially when the lure is being worked across the current or being activated by the rod tip. The hit is felt with a decided jar that is unmistakable. When small wet flies are used, line friction alone is enough and the fish hook themselves. In nymph fishing downstream, raising the rod tip smartly will often be all that is required at the moment the hit is felt.

Playing

Once the trout is hooked, a third of the battle is over and it is then a question of give and take that will come almost instinctively to most anglers. The fish makes a move and the angler counters; it should never be the reverse, for forcing at the wrong time can spell disaster, especially when light tackle is being employed.

This very disaster happened to me one May morning. Ernie and I waded side by side out into the Bridge Pool. My wet Cahill hooked a trout, and instantly the rod dove into an arc. The trout lashed forth to head for a fast run in midstream amid boiling water and big boulders. I figured him to slip downstream into a quiet pool, but he threw away the rules and remained where he was. Each time I tried to force him below he would hightail it upstream, so I finally waded down, hoping that eventually he would tire of the fast current. Suddenly he shot down the center, and I frantically gathered in the slack, though too much, for when he was forced to stop, up into the air he went, banged into the white foam and was gone, the barb still in his lip.

I do not believe exclusively in the taut-line school, for many trout are lost because of too tight a line. The more pressure is applied to the fish, the more he fights against it. To bear this out I recall watching an Oregon steelhead fisherman in action. The fellow had a nice fish on but was in a position where fighting him was difficult, and unless he moved to where he could operate better, he would surely lose him. As the angler started downstream to a beach below the rapids, he lowered his rod tip and slackened the line. The fish stopped working altogether, and only after the angler was all set in his new location and had tightened the line again was the battle resumed. I have employed this trick many times in Atlantic salmon fishing, when the big bruisers put a ledge, reef, or snag between myself and their position.

When does the line become too tight? Should a sizable trout make a sudden jab or run and no line is released, one of two things is going to happen. Either the hook will pull out of his mouth or something is going to break. If the leader is heavy and the trout big, it is liable to be the rod tip that snaps, or, failing that, a bamboo rod will acquire a "set." Any trout that is blamed for breaking a tip is falsely accused, and may the curses of the rod builder be upon the angler. The secret lies somewhere between too tight and too loose and can be found by controlling the slack and keeping a constant, though not heavy, pressure bend in the rod against the fish. The rod acts as the shock absorber. The second shock absorber is the line in the left hand. The correct use of this slack involves a technique seldom used except by well-schooled anglers.

When the trout makes a sudden run or lunge, release line but not enough to entirely relax rod pressure. Do not lower the rod tip. Should the trout turn and swim toward the rod, pull back on it to again establish the pressure. If necessary, line can be stripped in with the left hand.

A smart-alec rainbow can put you through your paces if he has been hooked downstream and suddenly decides to pick your legs as a hide-out! When he swims between your boots and jumps out of water behind, you are in a fix but good. Add to this his sudden turn downstream, wrapping the line around your leg and, to make matters still worse, jumping through a loop of slack line that is floating in front of you! I had to work out of this predicament last season, and it was all I could do to get untangled. As a matter of fact, I probably got into a worse tangle trying to free the line. Scotty got quite a kick out of watching me, and his guffaws started me laughing so hard that I almost lost my balance. I couldn't move my legs *or* reel in the line. How that fish ever stayed hooked, I'll never know, but thanks to Scotty's kind assistance, order was restored from this confusion and finally in his net reposed a plump rainbow that I really did not deserve—or did I?

Keep Him from Snags

It is easy to say "keep him from snags" but an entirely different thing to do it. It is a problem to be faced sooner or later in trout fishing. Browns and brooks invariably head for these locations when alarmed or hooked, and when they do, keep the pressure on the rod against them as best you can but always with the rod parallel to the water. This will help eliminate jumping.

If it is impossible to keep a hooked fish from brush or snags, relax all tension. Stop fighting for a moment, and the line will probably drift out into the open. If the fish does not swim clear, take in some line and walk over as close as you can get. Have the net in readiness and also keep a couple of yards of slack line held in the rod hand for a sudden dash. After managing to reach the fish, run your hand down the leader to inspect the situation. If the trout has wrapped the leader around some limbs and is still on, slip the net under him quietly, then get untangled. Trying to untangle first will cause more thrashing. Sudden pulls at this point are generally enough to snap all but the strongest leader.

There are times in big-stream angling when a fish will head for jagged rocks in order to file the leader. I can recall one trout in particular, a big she-rainbow that was hooked on a wet fly in mid-current well below me. She made a dash for the side water and up the shallows, dragging the line under a large boulder. Had I relaxed the line rather than use the rock as a pulley, I would have been all right. As it was, I was forced to wade down and reach underwater to loosen the line from the rock. When I resumed the battle I knew that it was only luck that she was still on.

The Jump

When the rod strain is constant, the fish will not be too tempted to jump. Even the saucy rainbow can usually be kept out of the air when handled without undue sudden strain, especially in the opening seconds of the battle. If and when he decides to jump, lower the rod tip immediately (or relax side strain) to about mid-point in order to give enough line quickly. Should he throw the hook while in the air, it generally means that too much line was given. If the leader breaks, not enough was given. This last can never happen if additional coils of line are readied and held in the left hand. It also pays to become very familiar with the action of the rod being used. If it is stiff, give more line, and if soft, give less.

Assuming for the moment that the trout does not throw the hook while in the air, snub him gently upon his return to the water, holding the loose line lightly in the left hand. Release a portion as he enters the water, and once he starts to run, set your rod instantly in a curve against him, parallel to the water, controlling the line as before. Gradually strip in line, but never relax rod pressure.

Netting the Trout

In most cases the netting of a fair-sized trout in average, not too fast water should not offer much of a problem. Guard against bringing in the fish before he is thoroughly played out and is turning on his side. When he comes in easily it does not take too much talent to run him into the submerged net and then scoop him up. When the fish is a big one and the conditions of netting are rough and your footing is none too secure, play the fish out and do not horse him through the fast water toward you unless you have a heavy leader, for the weight of the fish against the fast water will break even a strong leader, or the hook may pull out. The best plan of action is to move shoreward or maneuver into a bit of quieter water to which you can lead the fish. Often you can keep the fish in the heavy water while playing him and then wade to a logical spot, preferably below him, to do the final netting. This eliminates the necessity of reaching out ballet-dancer style, as shown in so many promotional angling photographs. Usually the angler is pictured with a sharply bent rod and net hand outstretched as if he was spearing something or was afraid to get near the fish for fear it would bite him! There is no reason for grandstand play in trout fishing. Bring the fish in close whether you are waist or ankle deep. Lead him into a quiet eddy and then into the net. Consider the net not as a thing to capture something wild but simply as a device by which you take in a played fish rather than use your hands. This concept in itself is the key to accident-free netting. In handling keeper fish and more especially the big ones it is always advisable to twist the net hoop to close the bag entrance once the fish is inside.

The question of leading the fish into the net head or tail first is a point that has been argued for years. If the fish is small and is to be returned it is always advisable to hand land him rather than run the risk of injury to the fins and scales. The smallish keepers can be handled either head or tail first, for when they're sufficiently played, it matters not. In the case of an exhibit fish, the choice depends upon the situation of the moment. Tail first is preferred by some because they are in the habit of getting below the fish in the current and either dropping the fish down into the net tail first, or bringing the net silently below and behind the fish while controlling his forward speed with the rod tip. The fish is enmeshed with a minimum of danger, and should he turn to make a sudden dash downstream, he would head right into the net. Others prefer to stand slightly upstream and net the fish head first. As fish like to swim against the current, the logic is that they will swim into the net when it is in front of them.

In either case, the main reason fish are lost is because the angler has failed to time the release of the line pressure to the exact instant the fish has entered the net. This results in the leader's banging against the net frame, thus holding the fish back from entirely entering the net.

Make it a point, especially when wading deep, to do the netting close to your body, thereby keeping your balance solid and motions quiet. Should you be in shallow and boulder-strewn water, do not go running after a fish or attempt to net him as he flops over the gravel. Don't swipe at him like a fencer. Relax the line pressure enough for him to swim into a hole, and then go over and take him out quietly.

Buy a good net for your particular purpose. Learn to use, carry, and care for it. Replace the net bag at least every two or three years whether you think it needs it or not. Examine the bag bottom occasionally to look for holes. When you find one, tie the loose ends together in an emergency and fix it up later. Before opening day it's a good practice to punch your closed fist into the bag and stretch it a bit. If it tears, there is still time to make a trip to the store.

A net that has become odorous from that well-known fishy smell is a mark that its owner knows how to fish but is hardly something to keep around the house as proof.

Washing will also preserve it. Comes wintertime, spend a little effort and revarnish the frame and check it over generally. Remember that even though you may not need the net very often, it should be there in easy reach and in perfect condition. Remember, too, that just because you have a net doesn't mean that you net or keep every fish you hook. Have fun with the fish and put a few back for next time.

Kill Instantly

The trout that you keep should be killed instantly, either by a blow of the net handle squarely across the butt of the head or by snapping the head back to break the neck. Clean them on the spot, removing the gills as well as the entrails. Don't wait for the digestive juices to go to work and cause the fish to become soft, mushy, and tasteless.

To Preserve

Wrap the trout individually in aluminum foil and stow them in your jacket creel or pouch. This maintains the original temperature and condition for many hours.

Conservation

I strongly and sincerely urge you to join Trout Unlimited and The Federation of Fly Fishers. These two organizations are doing much for the benefit of sport fishing, particularly trout fishing, in this age of destruction of our natural resources. These organizations are strong only because of the size of their memberships. The more people they can enlist who are interested in preserving and developing the art of fly fishing and raising the quality of trout waters, the more influence they can command. They are not trying to keep people out, and they *do not* look down on bait and spin fishermen. They can add two and two and get four. They can also subtract. They realize that many trout must remain in the stream if we are to have good fishing. In the fly-only and no-kill stretches of American trout streams one can find the best of angling. This is not true where bait and spin fishermen congregate. This is not to say that fly fishing methods are any less effective than the others. The fact is that a trout taken on bait will very likely die if released. Certainly a trout that takes a treble hook into its mouth will die when returned to the water. As proof of the top sport that intelligent management brings, try working fly-fishing-only no-kill stretches that are also restricted to barbless hooks! This last restriction was put there by the fly fishermen themselves as a further voluntary cutback on injured trout.

I wish you could fish the ranch property on Hot Creek in California. You'd see many trout there as long as your arm, and they can be caught too. The rule there is dry-fly fishing only (or a doped nymph if you prefer), a no-fish limit, and barbless hooks to be always used. That's an example of how it could be all over the map.

CHAPTER VI
A Stream of Thoughts and Memories

Streamside Sights and Sounds

It was one of those early April blue-sky days. The sun warmed my shoulders despite the chill winds that whistled down the river valley, ruffling the glides of the trout pools. The budding alders and brush fringing the banks and clinging to the rock-strewn cliffs were beginning to turn light green. Taller trees, blossoming in characteristic rusts and reds, stood out in bold contrast to the backdrop of somber evergreens not yet touched by a greening spring growth. Song sparrows twittered and hopped among the streamside willows and displayed their black-spotted breasts to the sun as they puffed their vibrating throats and gushed forth their familiar springtime jingles. Phoebes darted about, deftly snatching mayflies off the water and occasionally flitting to a standstill in midair to catch caddis flies as they rose straight up from the riffles. A robin warbled from its perch high in the elm that later, when its leaves were full, would shadow the tail of the pool. Far off on the hills a flock of crows was putting an owl to rout.

I was casting a brace of wet flies across a likely run of water. I waded along slowly, admiring the blue bonnets and violets shining on the banks amid the drabness of last year's fallen leaves. Here and there, among the rocks, windfalls, rotting tree stumps, and skunk cabbages, the pristine colors of other wild flowers glowed.

Anglers were working their rods both upstream and downstream from where I waded. I decided to give the water a good rest from the activity of the men who had just waded through. Besides, I was in no hurry. Who would be, on such a morning, when one feels content merely to be alive and on a trout stream. I sat on a rock with my rod across my knees and carried out the ritual of cleaning and filling my pipe. The woods seemed quiet enough, though the breeze swept dark splotches across the water. There was an uncertain, reserved quality in the songs of the birds. They, too, were merely visitors, come to feed, drink, and explore the streamside. Their mating time would come with the warmer days that were still a few weeks in the future.

The tobacco smoke tasted good. The wind quieted momentarily, and a ribbon of smoke drifted toward the branches of a great oak that canopied the edge of the stream. Many a time I had fished under the old landmark and had come to know it as a sheltering friend. My casual glance followed the smoke upward to where it dissolved into a dark blob of something foreign silhouetted against the sunlight. I remembered the contours of the branch well, and something had been added that was certainly not tree. A couple of blinks later I knew the answer. Quiet as you please, basking in the sun, and obviously missed by the parade of passing anglers, was a fat raccoon, seemingly fast asleep.

He didn't budge until I got up from the rock for a closer look. He knew then that he had been discovered. He wiggled his bearlike ears, twitched his berry-black nose, and opened his mouth to the sky for a long yawn. Then he looked down piercingly with those shoebutton eyes. Wading closer under the tree, I got a good look at him as he moved about unconcernedly.

Upstream about fifty yards three anglers were working their way down to us. I decided to try an experiment. I walked ashore, hardly glancing at the raccoon. I wanted to see whether any of the anglers coming down would spot the old codger. To make sure they would fish through the water, I sat well back on the bank in a position where I could watch the raccoon without being seen by the men.

One by one they came. The first man never looked up from his line as it went out rhythmically in downstream wet-fly casts. The second fished very deliberately, taking twice as long as the first to swim his flies in under the overhang, probably figuring that the still water beneath the tree would be a likely place to find a trout. The third man rushed along, sloppily wading and casting, hardly seeing anything. He seemed to be out more for the exercise than for anything else.

None of the three saw the coon. I am almost certain that they did not even hear the crows still worrying something. They did not see the chipmunk skirting the base of the old oak, nor did they spot me sitting close by in the brush, watching them.

I do not relate this incident to demonstrate my superior powers of observation, for I had noticed the coon only by chance, but merely to point out again that there's more to fishing than to fish. Trout country is full of surprises for those who will look for them.

Many other incidents outweigh in my memory the numbers of fish caught. I'm thinking now of a hair-raising event that happened suddenly one evening on the Esopus.

In early spring the lower reaches of the Esopus are a holding area for hordes of big rainbows, and at rare times it is possible to take them with dry flies. This particular evening had been a good one for me. I'd taken three big fish and was casting over another. My casting had become a bit mechanical. I was listening to a hermit thrush's organ-like warbling. The sound of the river was soothing.

Suddenly I heard a rushing windlike noise behind me. It had a frightening rhythmic pulse and was rapidly becoming louder. I turned and saw six Canada geese flying low and right at me. They looked like a flight of aircraft zeroed in on target. The few yards between us was rapidly evaporating. The lead gander honked the alarm, and the echelon broke in a clumsy confusion of rubbery necks and beating pinions as the geese tried simultaneously to break their speed and gain altitude. As soon as they had flashed over my head, they regained their formation, turned on their jets, and disappeared into the distance. I was sure they would not slow down until they had reached the middle of the broad expanse of the Ashokan Reservoir.

Another startling moment came about while I was fishing in northern Maine. I'd been quietly retrieving my wet flies through a deep backwater pond. I was hip-deep in the pool, not far from the high brushy bank. I was concentrating on fishing and was only dimly aware of the heavy crunch of something advancing toward the water. Then whatever it was was splashing into the water behind me. I snapped my head around and took in the ungainly snout and the massive antlers, still in velvet. There was nothing I could do to get out of the moose's way. I wished I possessed the magical talent of disappearing into thin air. He floundered halfway into the water and for a split second stood there glaring at me. I was at least as surprised as he was but managed a casual "hello."

That did it. He wheeled about and his long bulk mounted the bank. For a long time I could hear the sounds of his antlers crashing through the brush as he smashed his way deep into the timber.

Then, one day I had a brown creeper, a garter snake, and a grouse to lunch. I was parked comfortably against an old moss-covered windfall. The ancient spruce had fallen to just the right height to support my back, and I could lay my head against its softness and comfortably eat my sandwich and watch the stream at the same time. I was on the lookout for a friend who had promised to meet me at noon. We had planned it so that I'd fish up to the old tree and he would fish down to the meeting place.

As I sat munching, a brown creeper, one of those drab little avian insect eaters, walked head down along one side of the windfall, heading right toward me. He paused as he went around my head, then continued unalarmed along the moss to the next tree and proceeded up its trunk in his unbroken search for insects. I was glad that there had been no flies on my cap.

A minute later the leaves rustled next to me, and a small garter snake unwound itself out of the ground, looked me over briefly, and slithered across my leg and disappeared into the ferns.

Soon my angling partner appeared. I watched him work his way down the stream. I called to him, and he came into the shade for lunch. I had put my lunch bag against the windfall. As I reached for another sandwich and fumbled with the bag and its strap, my hand dropped to the leaves and my fingers felt something soft and feathery. I looked down and saw a ruffed grouse lying perfectly still, flattened in the leaves and blending into the ground cover. The bird had been there for a full half hour and had never moved. I lifted it up, and Frank's eyes almost dropped out.

"Nice having grouse for lunch, isn't it?" I said as the bird exploded away.

Many sights, sounds, and presences accompany a trout fisherman, for his stream is the ecological center, the lifeline, of woodland life. All my life I've enjoyed fleeting moments and amusing acquaintances with wild creatures. I've had a mink follow me down the stream, begging for the too numerous chubs I caught and running off with them one at a time into the brush, no doubt to feed his concealed family. I've watched as a fox stealthily seized and gobbled part of a hamburger that I'd left for a few moments on a rock. On another occasion I had a hefty black bear run me off from the trout I'd just cleaned, choose the two best, and lumber away into the woods, leaving me to nervously cook and eat my small remaining share. Once a praying mantis lit on my rod, flew to my hat, and spent the better part of an hour walking about on my shirt, down my sleeve, and back up my rod before fluttering away like a miniature helicopter. Woodchucks and porcupines have watched me fish, and jays and red squirrels have assembled and scolded me from the banks. I've always had a soft spot in my heart for the hated red squirrel. Have you ever been bawled out by a little red? These brief encounters with wildlife are but diverting incidents, but they are just the right additive to put a delightful finishing touch on a day's fishing.

Fisherman's Luck

Fishermen speak a good deal about luck. It's a term inextricably bound up with the sport, but what is luck really? Often it's no more than wishful thinking, and too often it's a substitute for hard work. Whether good or bad, luck is seen as an accident, something scarcely avoidable, and it seems man will usually consider luck what Webster calls "the chance happening of an event," whether it be the happy anticipation of a dream or an excuse for a failure. But there is more to ordinary luck than most people realize. Fishing as a sport provides an elaborate field laboratory for self-analysis. It can be an expansive drawing board upon which we can build a philosophy of living. What many of us strive to do in fishing we would all do well to attempt in everyday life—reduce luck, the chance element, to a minimum and fully realize that luck can be and frequently is the result of careful analysis and prolonged observation and strategy.

If we consider the story of the little boy and the cane pole, dime-store line, and bent pin, we find the real essence of luck in fishing. The boy, free from complex theories, traditions, and opinions, and with no significant record of failure to tell him how hard it is to catch fish, simply goes fishing, puts the bait where he expects fish to be, and catches some. The tall man, gray at the temples, sweating in chest-deep waders and bogged down with a couple of hundred dollars' worth of equipment, asks, "Where did you catch those beautiful trout and what did you take them on?" The boy's reply is simple and straightforward: "Under the shady side of the bridge, with a worm." What the boy didn't tell would fill volumes! He failed to mention just how many times he had fished the brook and how often he lay on the bridge, peering down at the water, studying all the signs of nature available to him. That string of trout the boy carries was not a lucky catch—he knows how to fish.

A master angler like Eddy Sens is not a lucky fisherman. Ed was born and raised on a trout stream and his thirst for perfection has kept him studying the mysteries of the current all his life. I have watched him take fish behind, in front of, and between hordes of other wading fishermen. And one could hardly call it luck. Ed belongs to the tiny community of experts who catch fish 99.9 per cent of the time. When you witness an angler take fish under seemingly impossible circumstances, you're quick to realize that luck is but a small measure of that kind of success.

Is it not the same in all endeavors? I know many radio, TV, and screen stars who have struggled relentlessly to get a "break." Yet the break was simply an incident in a long trail of experiences that made it comparatively easy to knock the big one over. A dressing-room confession from almost any star will reveal that without the experience, the grind, and at least a small portion of the heartbreaks, the so-called break wouldn't have presented itself. Their devotion to goals and their coolly thought-out strategy paid off in "the chance of a lifetime." Consider the scientist who suddenly discovers something of far-reaching significance. Luck? Oh, no! His discovery was the result of many years of burning the midnight oil and bearing the rigors of research. Without all that behind him, he would never have made the one last computation that solved the riddle.

It would seem, then, that if we all worked like busy little beavers, we could all become screen stars, board chairmen, or Einsteins—and we'd catch big fish every time out. This, of course, can never be. Not all fish grow to be record-breakers. Natural laws balance the scales, and in nature there is a reason for everything—floods, fires, depths, peaks, rocks, and rills. Yes, she designed blackflies and no-seeums for reasons other than to tax the angler's patience, just as she grows roses for reasons other than vain esthetics. No matter how brutal or beautiful, the breaks that come to people, places, and things are part of a plan.

Where does the fisherman fit into this plan? That's a complex question with a smoky answer, but our path is clear on one count. We must continue to flourish and progress while doing the best we can to perpetuate and improve the object of our love's labor, so succeeding generations can enjoy the great pleasures of sport fishing. Success can be a part of everyone's nature, and it can be made of many things; and who knows, we may find our objectives changing as we weigh the values of what we seek. One form of success in fishing is open to all—we can all work for sound conservation practices by approaching our sport in a truly sporting manner.

Outdoor Writers and Outdoorsmen

Years ago I worked as a radio announcer at CBS in New York City. I'd work long and hard hours all week, then escape for the weekend to the streams, woods, and fields. I used fishing and hunting as a dope. A good friend remarked one day that if I took dope or drank whisky as avidly as I fished and hunted, I'd end up in a ward in a matter of months.

When I left CBS for an agency job, another announcer did the same thing. We had fished together when we were at CBS, but now we found we had no time for it. One day we were playing cards on the commuter train to New York when I suddenly came to what I have realized since was a revelation.

"You know, John, one of us is nuts. We used to do a lot of hunting and fishing together when we had more time. Now we're successful executives, but we haven't fished or hunted together for a long time. Trout season opens this week, and neither of us is free to go."

His face took on a strange expression as I continued my tirade.

"You know, a two-week vacation to do what you really want to do is a lousy return on your money. Two from fifty-two! Today I'm quitting, and I'm going to move to Florida."

"Before you make any such gestures as that, perhaps you had better take a vacation," he remarked, as we prepared for the pushing contest in the subway. But I was firm in my resolve. I really threw in the sponge.

Yes, my, how our values change. Today, as an outdoor writer who has not been on a salary for twenty years, I consider myself very lucky. I can hunt when I like, fish when I like, and enjoy all the intangibles, the pleasures of which I write here—the events, places, times, people, and feelings that linger and sustain one throughout a lifetime of playful seasons. You don't make a fortune as an outdoor writer, but you can live fifty-two weeks of the year, for even writing about the outdoors is a pleasure.

I don't mean to imply that the outdoor writer's life is all peaches and cream. There's a lot of work involved, and once you're in print you're considered an expert by many, and at times this evaluation is a difficult one to live up to. The job carries many responsibilities. Readers and friends expect you to have instant, accurate know-how and information at your fingertips. Experts of the rod-and-gun clubs love to assert their egos, and sometimes long debates must be carried to a victorious finish or the king of the castle is toppled.

One cogent definition of an expert is "a guy far away from home." Another I've always liked, partly because it was formulated by my good friend Ed Zern, is this: "An expert is one with whom you go fishing and if nobody catches anything, knows all the reasons why." Ed is a Pennsylvania Dutch Quaker and Madison Avenue advertising executive. He is a tragedian at heart, though he expresses himself in a most extraordinary way as a humorist. One of his astute observations is that people named Ray seem drawn to out-door expression, and to back up his premise he mentioned Ray Bergman, long-time fishing editor of *Outdoor Life* and author of *Trout, Bass,* and other well-known books. Next on the list was Ray Shenkheisen, for many years editor of the "1001 Outdoor Questions" on the back page of *Field & Stream,* of which Ray Holland was then editor. Ray Camp is of course well known for his books and magazine articles and for the New York *Times*'s daily column "Wood, Field, and Stream," which he wrote for a number of years. The well-known outdoor and nature artist Don Ray can be included. And then there's Ray Trullinaer, my predecessor at the *World-Telegram & Sun*'s "Hooks and Bullets" column.

There are a host of outdoor writers in the business of dispensing news of sporting events, conservation, and how-to and where-to information on all phases of the outdoors. With some good reason these men are often accused of being ne'er-do-wells who are unable to earn an honest living at a regular job, preferring to goof off at hunting and fishing and hiding behind the label of expert authority. They are often jealous of one another, though they're most friendly on the surface on such occasions as when Winchester throws a big shindig at a shooting preserve. Ed Zern once said that these parties are great fun, but just make sure when you are hunting in the field that you know who is shooting behind you. The market for articles is much smaller than the crop of supplying writers.

Now, just what is it that makes a writer an expert? Is it that he can express himself and some editor has bought his words? I've known men and a few women in my life who have been so much a part of nature and the outdoors that they have forgotten more than most writers will ever know. They are the real experts, but unfortunately they cannot or do not write. Take Aaron, for example, a forest ranger in the Catskills. I've spent many hours with him in the woods. He is a human representative of the wilds. He knows all the tricks of living off the country, and could survive easily if all contact with humankind was denied him. He's an experienced woodsman, tracker, dog trainer, searcher and finder of lost persons, and weather and season prophet. There is little that this man could add to his knowledge of the outdoors, yet he is unpublished, and therefore is virtually unknown. It is the same the world over in all kinds of categories. People seem to think that a person is an expert merely because he is published somewhere.

I'm sure one of the most serious gaps in our cultural and educational system is that between the capable writer and the inhibited expert. If the knowledgeable ones were to come out in print more often, we'd be a shade better off. Also, too often the person with the influence dictates who shall write and what he will say. There are numerous examples of this, particularly in the battles over conservation and the citizens' right-to-bear-arms issue, to mention only two.

I wish there were more who are what I would call true experts. Jack O'Connor is one in the guns and hunting field and is one of the few this writer has really looked up to. Lee Wulff is another in the fields of general hunting and fishing, and certainly Ray Bergman was another, along with Roderick Haig-Brown, Van Campen Heilner, and the late John Alden Knight. Their books have lived over many years. The usual sale of an outdoor book is small compared with the effort and time it took to write it, but their books have earned royalties over the years because the information they contain is sound and well expressed. Their success is a model for others to follow.

In company with Ray Nelson, Larry Koller, and Guy Kibbee, I had the opportunity to interview "on the air" more than two hundred outdoor writers over a fifteen-year period on the Mutual Radio Network's "Rod and Gun Club of the Air," one of the few programs that ever outrated a presidential broadcast. These experts were fun to deal with. Most were egotistical, believing that only they knew all the secrets. Nelson and Koller often went to work on them and cut some inflated reputations down to size, but the aggregate of what those experts brought to the show was a broad and tremendously valuable source of outdoor lore, tips, and hints. Written down, this information would have made several remarkable volumes.

Larry showed through the years on the program that he was an expert loaded for bear when it came to instantly retrievable knowledge of the outdoors. His expertise had been developed by years of experience in the wilds and in the shop. I first knew Larry when he was a gunsmith in Poughkeepsie, New York. There was a time in his life when he was forced to poach game and fish in order to feed his family. In those years Larry acquired a knowledge of the outdoors that was to become invaluable. Much of this he passed on to his readers. Now, Larry did not consider himself a writer or an expert, at least not until his later years, but anyone who has read *Shots at Whitetails* would consider him a master of his profession. His *Taking Larger Trout* is also a classic. Yet Larry's education and natural bent was to anything but writing. He'd rather have spent his time drinking and carousing than pinning himself down to a typewriter. He was a strange combination of diverse personalities. He lived high and hard through the horrible days of poverty and into the cream of an outdoor writer's success.

Here's an example of Larry's fishing prowess. He and five other writers were fishing the Allagash River in Maine. Now, much to the embarrassment of the Maine publicity bureau, the brook trout do not grow big in Maine, not as big as they used to, anyway. That day, fishing in various ways, including the use of worms, we all took nice strings of small trout. Larry was the last to show up for a cookout we'd planned. He had gone downstream without the guide, and when he appeared on the scene we all felt like bowing. Gilled in his fingers were two of the prettiest monster brook trout ever to come out of Maine or anywhere else. They both weighed over four pounds.

I've fished with Larry on his pet water, the lower Neversink in the southern tier of the Catskills. There are some very big brown trout in that part of the river, and they grow big simply because they're just about impossible to catch. But Larry could catch them. I wish I'd been able to make movies of him at work, so I could show how he did it. Much of his experience and advice is to be found in *Taking Larger Trout,* and I confess to lifting many of his teachings for some of my own books.

Talk of outdoor experts always makes me think of Jim Deren, an expert in many fields if ever there was one. Jim is the long-time proprietor of the Angler's Roost, a small but impressive and historic tackle shop that was for many years located in the basement arcade of the Chrysler Building. There is virtually nothing that Jim doesn't know about outdoor tackle and equipment. Many well-known authorities have haunted the Roost, seeking the tips and information that Jim gives so freely. Jim is an expert in human relations too. By just being himself—one minute gracious, the next a gut-busting humorist, at another time a serious discusser of the downfall of the human race, sometimes a drinker and carouser, and always one of the best woodsmen any of us will ever know—he generates a magic of the ingratiating kind that simply melts people and makes them love him, sometimes in spite of themselves. To that little store the greats of the outdoor world come to discuss their plans, ideas and projects. Jim looks at them in a kindly way, asks a few questions, and for some magical reason they go away with confidence in their ideas. Jim would be considered by many therapists to be in need of couching himself, but he is a great calmer. Many of us weary Madison Avenue "executives" would spend our lunch hours hanging around the Roost, not knowing quite why. I was the most fortunate. My office was three floors above his ceiling. After about two o'clock, the club would disperse and we'd return to the office refreshed and happy with the grim world again. The Roost was always full of experts who came for whatever it was, and few of them bought much tackle.

Stu Longendyke, a good looking young fly tier and budding expert himself, took over as Jim's assistant. Without Stu, Jim might have gone broke. Stu knew when and when not to bring out the prize hackle necks that made the Roost famous. He kept his eye on them and on the fingering customers. Stu couldn't have made a fortune working for Jim, yet he stayed and was Jim's most loyal friend and helper.

This writer was completely taken over by Guru Deren. I had been a hunter and fisherman all my life, but just being around Jim turned on certain energies that seemed to push me into being an experimenter, outdoor student, and finally a writer. While we were discussing wet-fly fishing one day, Alan Anderson, then New York editor of Little Brown and Co., came in to purchase some fly leaders. The three of us got to talking, Jim's magic began to take hold, and ten minutes later Alan decided to look seriously at a book on wet-fly and nymph fishing that Jim thought I should and could write.

After Alan left for his office, I said to Jim, "For God's sake, you know what you have got me into? I can't in any degree of honesty write that book. Sure I can catch some trout on wets and nymphs and tie up a few patterns, but write a book?"

As if by magic, Ed Sens walked in, and we were introduced. Ed is one of those little-known experts I spoke about earlier. He has spent his life soaking up nature. He's a descendent of an early New York Dutch family that continued to hold an ancient grant to a choice bit of property in the Catskills. The Neversink River carved out some magnificent pools on his land, and they had story-book trout in them, including some bigger-than-wilderness brookies.

Ed later showed me the spot where an old covered bridge had once spanned the stream. He'd cross this bridge on his way back from school and always spend a few minutes peering down at the stream between the cracks in the timbers. He'd see trout, big ones, and study them. Throughout those years Eddy acquired fishing gear and learned the art of fly tying. He observed the cycle of the season, the series of insect hatches, the changes of light, water currents and levels, and the general movements of the trout. He came to know intimately the life of a trout stream. Much of Ed's know-how formed the basis of the first edition of this book.

After several seasons of fishing those Neversink waters and other streams with Ed, and taking lessons from him in the fine art of fly tying, I wrote this book in the offices of the Birmingham, Catleman and Pierce advertising agency, where I was supposed to be in charge of a million dollars of billing annually. My secretary was a quick-change artist. She'd be typing business papers one minute and then during slower periods would shift over to my manuscript. So I really owe my writing career to Jim.

Jim loves the Beaverkill. He has wept at the sight of the "progress" that has afflicted this wonderful stream over the years as the Army Corps of Engineers and the road builders wreaked their havoc. Yet, Jim himself did little about it, even though we all tried to get him to write and speak out.

He was more valuable in the role of goading others to do the editorial shouting. His mission was that of the man behind the scenes. Though he'd never take credit for it, Jim was responsible for forming the Bemoc Club, a group of Metropolitan anglers and owners of camps and homes along the course of the Beaverkill and its tributary, the Willowemoc. Walt Dette and Harry Darbee, two famous fly tiers who have lived their lives on the river, were charter members.

I'd heard and read about the Beaverkill for many years but somehow had never fished it. One week-end Jim took me for a tour of the river. It was quite an experience, for along the way he related many unwritten and little-known anecdotes from the lives of such early Catskill anglers as Theodore Gordon, George La Branch, and Pop Robbins. I believe that someday, someone will write a book that will tell in all its glory the story of the Beaverkill as a part of Americana as important in its way as many of our national shrines.

It was about a week after the tour that I spotted the Deren hat while fishing the Junction Pool, where the Willowemoc joins the Beaverkill. Jim's hat is a trademark. You can spot it a mile away, covering that large head that sits somewhat snugly on large, drooping shoulders. Jim's big and tall, and he fishes slowly, like a poacher. I watched Jim land and release four big trout, two browns and two rainbows. He was using big wet flies tied by Larry Koller. He had wrapped enough wrap-around lead to the leader to sink the works down to the bottom of the ocean in a fast tide. His technique was to drag the bottom where the big ones would get the drift.

The display window of the Roost was merely a disorderly extension of the confusion of dusty tackle inside the shop. The dust was so thick that I wondered if Jim secretly

brought it in every morning and blew it around for atmosphere. Waders and rod bags hung from the ceiling, the
tackle shelves were in constant disarray, and nobody knew
the price of anything. The book section was crammed with
a good many first editions, which were read out loud but not
sold. There were also books for sale, many on fly-tying, for
that is Jim's sales forte. Liz Gregg, the well-known Scottish
tier was a good friend and added to the Roost's appeal as a
sit-in teacher. There was a small table in the corner of the
store where the fly-tying light was always lit. Someone was
usually sitting there, either a beginner or an expert tying
flies to a standing audience. People would wander in and
out, looking curiously at the unceremonious confusion that
was oddly situated in this formal arcade in the world's
second-tallest building. That kind of unorganized mess was
just not in keeping with the Madison Avenue spirit. And
Jim did not dress like a salesman, or even like a gentleman.
Sometimes he shaved and usually he wore a soiled T-shirt,
but the gray-flannel clan loved him.

Jim's steady customers are a varied lot. Advertising-
agency art directors come to Jim to arrange authentic and
technically correct tackle settings and layouts for ads that
call for the outdoor motif. Fishing editors such as Al
McClane of *Field & Stream* have sometimes sought Jim's
advice. Such artists as Lynn Bogue Hunt, Paul Bransom,
Charles De Feo, and William Shaldach haunted the place.
Jim is credited with starting many of today's best fly tiers
in the business. He is consulted by rod companies on matters of tackle design. Book publishers kept him busy reading
manuscripts.

One of Jim's weaknesses is youngsters. If a young boy
came in and nervously spent a little money, Jim would heap
him with articles that he could not buy but would sorely
need, all free of charge. Once in a while he'd trade gear, and

a sharper trader you've never seen. At other times he would detail sales slips and even add the tax, refuse credit, and even refuse to take a check. He treated some roughly, others like his own mother.

Few outdoor experts and outdoor writers will ever begin to approach the knowledge of Deren. Since becoming a writer I have sometimes been referred to as an expert, but frankly the label is embarrassing, and I do not consider it to be merited. In Jim's case, though, the label is perfectly apt. He is an expert's expert.

There's a select group of outdoor writers who lunch together in the caverns of New York City. They used to meet at the truly fabulous Laughton Carver Restaurant. I've attended several of their lunches, which consist mainly of a bunch of story-tellers all trying to upstage each other. But there was one real expert outdoor writer in that bunch, and he had a profound effect on all of us. I'm thinking of Jack Randolph, "John" in his column for the New York *Times*. For half a century Jack held down editorial jobs of the highest order in the newspaper business. In his later years, when he was in what might be called semiretirement, he took on the daily stint of the "Wood, Field & Stream" column for the *Times* after Ray Camp's long tenure. To follow Camp they *had* to get a good one.

Jack was an exception to all the rules. First of all, he knew far more about the art of writing than any of us would ever learn. He had a sense of humor that had nothing to do with promoting himself in the career-minded braggadocio-oriented world of outdoor writing. He plagued and razzed his colleagues, and they begged for more because it was good publicity. Those who really went after Jack, hoping for a mention in his column, never reached print. Jack was an exceptional reporter when necessary—a cool, calm, analytical observer with years of newsdesk training. But he could raise fire in his readers over almost any issue of the day, and all the while there was fun and frolic in his writing, no matter how serious the subject became.

One fond remembrance I have of Jack was the time the American Forest Products Industry representative in New York invited me to the Allagash Region in Maine. At that time Washington was interested in grabbing it away from the lumber barons "before it was too late." I called Jack on the phone, since he had just returned from an outdoor trip there. I asked him if he would like to return with me as the guest of the organization that represented the barons, and he promptly agreed.

Well, you should have seen and heard how he treated these public-relations men at the briefings at various points along the way. These men were used to the average outdoor writer, who was eager to dine on steaks and good liquor, enjoy an outing, and then go back to the desk and peddle the product. In his polite way Jack cut them down as to the motive behind the whole affair and its position of industry self-interest. He asked them some very embarrassing questions that showed he was a man of acute penetration and not afraid of anyone or of the issues at stake. Yet it was all done smoothly and politely. But the columns he delivered showed that the very possessive self-interest of the lumber people was a good guarantee of future forests and a continually changing ecological pattern that would benefit wildlife.

He appeared in his subtle way to be exposing the frauds of the PR fraternity, which made good reading, but he was all the while pointing up the sound management practices of the lumber companies.

During that trip he remarked that the steaks were always too well done and that even an amateur PR man should listen and act when he was asked for a *rare* steak. One of the team mentioned this complaint to me, and I suggested a plan that would surely knock the old eagle over. The dinner that night took place on an island camp, in a lush log cabin complete with all the down-East wilderness atmosphere. The guides had evidently been told not to shave and to wear their traditional plaid shirts and hunting boots. The place looked like something out of a movie location. When dinner was announced we advanced on the big dining room, and Jack was seated at the head of the table. He didn't choose the spot. By prearrangement it was the only chair available. One by one the sizzling steaks were brought in and placed before us. His was the last to come. While I'm sure he noted this fact, there was not a shred of recognition on his face or in his actions, but those who know Jack are aware that nothing ever goes by him in any direction unnoticed. The wait simply allowed him time for another drink. When the chef finally brought in Jack's platter, on it was a steak two inches thick and as raw as the day it was hacked off the bone. Jack hardly looked down as he automatically cut the meat and ate it with an air of complete composure. We all watched with fascination as he finished every bit of that tremendous hunk of meat. It was a miracle that we were able to hold back our laughter. The PR men went crazy over him, and the tensions disappeared.

Reflections on "Progress"

It is evident that man as he evolves is being forced into a vortex of pressures he himself has concocted. The values of a generation ago are not necessarily those which this generation appreciates. When we used horses instead of cars, we had few roads, and wilderness abounded. Now wilderness, and native trout, belong to a bygone era in most parts of this country. This unhappy fact reminds me of a

casual lecture on "progress" I once heard. It came from the lips of one who has a sharp quality of getting right to the point. He and I were in New Brunswick on a salmon trip. Our camp was primitive, without indoor plumbing. There was no hurry to get to the river. It had been raining for five days and the river was overflowing its banks. So what do people do when they can't be active? They think. All the energy converges in the brain.

It was during this idle time that he began:

"Progress, bah! What has man gained in the past fifty years? Quality? True progress? No. Television—and frightened little hatchery trout. What has he gained since the demise of the outhouse? First, he was elevated to the era of the unpainted and then the painted birch johnny seat, and he figured he was getting somewhere. Now he has all sorts of fancy indoor plumbing. But you know what he lost when the old rustic monument to courage and fortitude went by the evolutionary boards?

"The trout. The big, fat, honest, stream-bred trout and the clear, cold streams that had never seen a bulldozer, a real-estate salesman, or a sign painter. Trout then reached the three and four pound mark, and you had to bend them to fit them into a creel. About all you could carry would be two or three. And you could catch them within an easy walk from the cabin.

"So what happened? We got birch johnny seats and hard-topped roads so that the heavy trucks could deliver the plumbing, and we ended up with more fishermen and smaller trout. That's why I prefer outside plumbing. But despite the forward march of civilization, with its fancy indoor plumbing, I would gladly trade all the modern conveniences for even the medium-sized trout. I'd be glad to go back to the badly potted, old tire-killing roads if that would bring back the trout.

"Progress? We have air-conditioned motels, with indoor plumbing facilities, that cost—for one night—more than I used to earn in a week, and all that is left of the trout are a few mangy ones mounted on stained cratewood that's supposed to give an illusion of rugged backwoodsiness. The resort publicity boys write about the fine trout fishing, but they avoid mention of the catching.

"I must also confess a hunger for the sort of eventful drive to a trout stream where I might have to pause to let a moose go by or a bear cross in front, or strain my neck looking through the rear window as I back up a quarter of a mile to let the warden pass. I'd like to careen over rutty roads between clay mires on both sides, the kind that used to lure me into the muck clear up to the running boards. I'd like one right now, muddy and hazardous in a downpour of spring rain, because I know it would lead to baking-sized trout.

"My old lady, bless her, who among other things knew the art of cooking trout as none of her grandchildren do, would give me a parting warning about the curves and the ditches, as I'd leave the porch with my rod poked under my arm. Would she fuss now as I fly over the six-laners that have intruded upon the pastures behind her house? I can't bear those sleep-drugged curves designed to keep speeding idiots safe in their streamlined tin cans while their minds have succumbed to rock-and-roll, ball games, and radio talk shows. When it comes to peace and quiet and trout—big trout—give me one of those long-gone country roads with pole-timber bridges over spring brooks where you had to slow down to a stop rather than fly as you do over the forbidding modern concrete bridges that offer naught but stream disruption and cement drippings. Besides, the new roads and their bridges lead to nowhere except progress.

"I have a practical and sentimental attachment to the memory of my old car with its crank up front. That was the kind of car that was made in an era when men were men and women, women, a far cry from the situation of today when you can't tell one from the other on the street. My kind of car was made with care, loving care, during an age of responsibility and close tolerances, when there were no income-tax forms requiring a battery of CPA's to keep me out of jail.

"There are many other valuable things that have been lost down the modern drain. For example, many people nowadays warn against loaning valuables. Now that attitude is a sick sign of the times—but, you know, they are right. There are only a few souls left who I would lend my tackle to, and they are dying off fast.

"I've come to the point where I can't stand crowds and will be content to avoid highway ditches full of gas and oil run-offs and stocked with faded, undersized trout.

"And you know what?" my friend concluded. "All this tribulation has all come about because some idiot became huffy about the coldness of the john on some early spring excursion into God's country. Had he worn his red underwear that morning instead of figuring a way to move the john inside to the warmth, all this mess could have been avoided."

Well, certainly we can't go back to the old double holer; we can only march ahead. Whether the trout will continue to grow smaller and fewer depends on whether we can find a balance of values and translate this into what can be called progress in the true sense. History shows that only when things have gotten really bad has man been able to wake up and do something. In a way, we can be thankful for the smog, for everybody's eyes are burning now, not just the trout fishermen's! According to some scientists, it is just a matter of time before we will be wearing gas masks to and from air-conditioned homes and places of work. If this comes about, where will we go to hunt and fish and surf and boat?

My son is approaching his tenth year. A few minutes ago, before I sat down to type these last words, he asked me what would happen if the whole earth became polluted like Los Angeles. "Would we all die?" he asked, and before I could answer, he went on, "and would there be any fish left to catch?"

As I looked down at his innocent face and inquisitive eyes, I suddenly saw my life in the out-of-doors pass in review. I saw my father in the stern seat of a canoe, guiding me on the water on my tenth birthday and showing me how to paddle. Up until the day dad passed away he revered the streams, the fields, and the wilds of the oceans, forests, and mountains. He laid on me the responsibility to help preserve those values and natural heritages. "Lose them, and you have lost everything. Nature is bountiful but no respecter of violators," he had warned.

At the moment when my son asked that question, I knew that, if the prophets of ecological doom were right, I had failed him. I wondered just how many years my son would have left to live, much less have an outdoors to go to. I asked myself, "What have I given him after bringing him into the world?"

In all holy scriptures, the shadow of doom always brings with it the condition that man must eventually turn to principle and truth—or else. The truth in nature is eternal and available to all who have eyes to see. The businessmen have failed us. The technologists have failed us. To whom (or what) can we turn?

In Biblical terms, man has been granted "dominion over"

the planet Earth. He has ruthlessly altered the face of the earth to meet his changing needs. But the time is past when we could interpret our "dominion" as taking the form of willful exploitation. It is becoming ever more clear that man is only a part of nature, not the absolute ruler of it. We have a place and a role in nature, and our role cannot be that of the disinterested manipulator. We cannot be disinterested, because what we do to nature is more and more coming to rebound on ourselves, to our great disadvantage. If we have failed in the past to respect and maintain our natural heritage, now we must act to restore it or suffer the impending consequences. The responsibility cannot be left for future generations. It is virtually the eleventh hour. We can all take a part in making the population in general, and our civic and political leaders in particular, aware that the crisis exists and daily grows more extreme, and that it affects *them*. We can all take a part, however small, in delaying or halting the excessive depletion of our resources and the pollution of our water, earth, and air. We can all strive to change our ways of life and views of the world to practices and attitudes that are more functional, more adaptive, and more stable. The forests, the air, the waters—*and* the big trout—can all be brought back to something like their former glory, but only if we all lend a hand. Man has been given the power to change the face of the earth. Must he change that wonderful face into a painful scowl?